cooking for
ONE

cooking for
ONE

Over **90** delicious recipes
that prove one can be fun

RYLAND PETERS & SMALL
LONDON • NEW YORK

Designer Barbara Zuñiga
Production Controller Meskerem Berhane
Art Director Leslie Harrington
Editorial Director Julia Charles
Publisher Cindy Richards

Indexer Hilary Bird

First published in 2015 by
Ryland Peters & Small
20–21 Jockey's Fields
London WC1R 4BW
and
341 E 116th St.
New York, NY 10029

www.rylandpeters.com

All text (other than those recipes credited
on page 144), design and photographs
© Ryland Peters & Small 2015

ISBN: 978-1-84975-602-0

10 9 8 7 6 5 4 3 2 1

A CIP record for this book is available from
the British Library.

US Library of Congress Cataloging-in-
Publication data has been applied for.

Printed and bound in China

NOTES

- Both British (Metric) and American (Imperial plus US cups) are included in these recipes for your convenience, however it is important to work with one set of measurements and not alternate between the two within a recipe.
- All spoon measurements are level, unless otherwise specified.
- All herbs used in these recipes are fresh, unless otherwise specified.
- All eggs are medium (UK) or large (US), unless specified as large, in which case US extra-large should be used.
- When a recipe calls for the grated zest of citrus fruit, buy unwaxed fruit and wash well before using. If you can only find treated fruit, scrub well in warm soapy water before using.
- Ovens should be preheated to the specified temperatures. We recommend using an oven thermometer. If using a fan-assisted oven, adjust temperatures according to the manufacturer's instructions.
- Any leftover rice from these recipes can be stored in the fridge but must not be kept for longer than 1 day. Reheat in the microwave until piping hot. Leftover rice can also be frozen. Cool quickly and freeze in individual portions. Defrost in the fridge and reheat thoroughly in the microwave, again, until piping hot.
- Recipes containing prawns/shrimp or other seafood should be eaten fresh on the day they are made and should not be kept. It is not always possible to be sure that prawns, even if fresh, have not been previously frozen. If practical to do so, freeze portions of the sauce without the prawns/shrimp and simply add them fresh when you next make the recipe.

introduction 6

introduction

It's easy to underestimate the pleasures of cooking for just one person – you. But you can experiment and adapt recipes however you like because nobody else's tastes need to be catered for. Dinner will be ready when you are; and there's no better way of looking after yourself and giving yourself a treat than taking the time to prepare and enjoy something good to eat.

Don't be tempted to take shortcuts just because you're only cooking for one person. Whether you're looking forward to a quick, comforting midweek supper in front of the TV, or something more special after a long week at work – when you'll sit at the table, get out the linen napkins and nice plates and pour yourself a glass of wine – enjoy taking time over your meal.

Of course, cooking for one comes with its own challenges; see over the page for practical suggestions for how to get round these. Some recipes, such as soups, stews and most baked goods, are best made in two or more servings, but they can be stored in the fridge and served the next day with something different, or frozen to eat a few weeks later. It can be tricky to buy some ingredients in small quantities, but with a little ingenuity they can often be used in many different ways; a well-stocked basic storecupboard will help here.

It's important to include enough variety in your diet when you're cooking for one, but it means you can experiment as much as you like, with no one to please but yourself!

Whether you are living alone all or part of the time, working shifts, or flat sharing and catering just for yourself most of the time, cooking for one can be economical, practical and enjoyable. All that's required is some planning, shopping and forethought.

cooking for one is fun!

stock up on storecupboard essentials

A well-stocked storecupboard makes it easy to ring the changes with your favourite fresh ingredients. Good-quality oils, vinegars and mustards are essential for homemade dressings, along with a range of herbs and spices to experiment with. Grow pots of fresh herbs on your windowsill to avoid buying packets you won't use up, and look out for tubes of fresh herb pastes that are now available in many stores.

Different types of dried pasta, noodles, rice, lentils and pulses/legumes are useful, as are canned tomatoes, tuna, beans, olives, anchovies and artichokes. Eggs, yogurt and cheese all keep well in the fridge and are multi-taskers that will ensure you have a tasty supper on the table in no time; a range of sauces, condiments, pickles and spice rubs is also handy. If you need alcohol for a recipe, consider buying miniatures.

make the most of leftovers

With a bit of lateral thinking you can convert any leftovers into a different, tasty meal the next day. Chilli con carne, ragù and other meat stews will keep for a few days in the fridge, and are delicious as a baked potato filling or served with rice or couscous.

Leftover pasta or cooked root vegetables are delicious when fried gently with beaten eggs, cheese and chopped herbs in a frittata; leftover cooked rice can be re-purposed in

stir-fries or egg-fried rice; leftover cooked vegetables can be coarsely crushed, bound with egg and fried in olive oil as fritters to serve with your favourite condiment.

make good use of your freezer

Freeze leftovers, clearly labelled with the date, in single-size portions so that you can easily defrost only what you need. The freezer is a great place to store tortillas, flatbreads, regular bread, bagels and muffins (remember to slice them before freezing), which can be toasted straight from frozen. Bread that has gone stale can be whizzed into breadcrumbs and stored in the freezer to use as a topping for gratins or coating for fritters, and egg whites can also be frozen individually.

Think of your freezer as a useful extension to your storecupboard: frozen peas, green beans, spinach, prawns/shrimp, berries and pastry are all extremely versatile stand-bys.

cook in batches

Although many recipes are straightforward to make for one person, some are easier to make in larger quantities and store for future use, so it's often wise to make more than you need. Baked goods like muffins and small cakes freeze well once baked; biscuit/cookie doughs can be frozen raw and baked as you need them; muesli and granola can be made in bulk and kept in an airtight container for a couple of weeks.

Most homemade spice rubs, dressings and marinades, tricky to make in small quantities, will keep well if covered with a layer of oil in a sealed jar in the fridge. Keep homemade burgers, shaped but not cooked, in the freezer. A whole roast chicken or joint of beef can form the basis of many different meals, from soups to salads to sandwiches.

chapter 1

start the day

satisfying breakfasts and brunches

Making your own granola is a great way to control what is going into your breakfast cereal. It's easy to do and you can make a large batch and store it in an airtight container for a couple of weeks.

granola with berry compote

500 g/5 cups rolled oats

150 g/1⅛ cups mixed chopped nuts

150 g/1¼ cups mixed seeds

50 g/¾ cup desiccated/dried shredded coconut (optional)

½ teaspoon salt (optional)

2 teaspoons mixed/apple pie spice

2 eating apples, grated with skin on

2 tablespoons dark brown sugar

4 tablespoons vegetable, sunflower, canola or hazelnut oil

8 tablespoons runny honey, maple syrup or golden/light corn syrup

150 g/1 cup chopped mixed dried fruit of your choice

plain yogurt, to serve

For the berry compote

300 g/3 cups blackberries, blueberries and raspberries (fresh or frozen)

6 tablespoons honey or golden/light corn syrup

1–2 tablespoons brown sugar

freshly grated zest of 1 lemon

freshly squeezed juice of ½ lemon

1 cinnamon stick or ½ teaspoon ground cinnamon (optional)

1 teaspoon vanilla extract

Makes 8 servings

Preheat the oven to 150°C (300°F) Gas 2.

Put the oats, nuts, seeds, coconut, salt (if using) and mixed/apple pie spice in a large mixing bowl, add the apple and stir until well combined.

Put the sugar, oil and honey in a saucepan set over low heat and stir until melted. Pour over the dry ingredients and stir until the mixture is well combined.

Spread out the mixture evenly on the largest baking sheet you have, taking care not to heap the mixture to ensure that it cooks evenly. Bake in the preheated oven for 40–45 minutes, stirring every 10 minutes, until the granola is golden. Then add the dried fruit and bake for a further 5 minutes. If you can, watch the mixture quite closely in the oven to make sure that it does not burn.

To make the berry compote, put all the ingredients in a saucepan and set over low-medium heat. Simmer gently until the fruit has softened but is still holding its shape and the liquid has reduced. Turn off the heat and leave to cool. The compote will keep in a jar in the fridge for a week.

Allow the granola to cool and then store it in an airtight container until ready to eat. Serve each portion with a large spoonful each of plain yogurt and berry compote.

Leftover berry compote will keep in a sterilized jar in the fridge for up to 2 weeks or can be frozen in small portions – an ice cube tray works well – and defrosted when needed. It can be used for the French Toast recipe on page 16 or makes a delicious topping for scoops of vanilla ice cream.

These muffins are a fantastic grab-and-go midweek breakfast and contain lots of fruit, nuts and fibre to keep your energy levels high all morning. They are perfect for batch baking and freezing.

honey and apricot breakfast muffins

200 g/1½ cups plain/all-purpose flour

½ teaspoon bicarbonate of soda/baking soda

2½ teaspoons baking powder

2 teaspoons mixed/apple pie spice

50 g/½ cup chopped dried apricots

50 g/½ cup pecan nuts, chopped, plus extra for topping

100 g/1 cup porridge oats

50 g/½ cup sultanas/golden raisins

2 bananas (preferably soft)

2 unpeeled apples, grated

2 eggs

5 tablespoons vegetable oil

1 teaspoon vanilla extract

4 tablespoons honey

6 tablespoons milk

100 g/½ cup light brown sugar

a 12-hole muffin pan, lined with muffin cases

Makes 12 (the rest can be frozen for later)

Preheat the oven to 180°C (350°F) Gas 4.

Sift the flour into a mixing bowl. Add the bicarbonate of soda/baking soda, baking powder and mixed/apple pie spice and stir to combine. Add the dried apricots, pecans and oats to the flour mixture together with the sultanas/golden raisins and set aside.

In a separate bowl, mash the bananas with a fork. Add the apples, eggs, oil, vanilla extract, honey and milk and stir to combine. Add the sugar and stir again.

Make a well in the centre of the dry ingredients. Pour in the wet ingredients and gently stir from the centre, gradually drawing in the dry ingredients to make a smooth batter.

Fill the muffin cases two thirds full and top with chopped pecans for added texture. Bake in the top half of the preheated oven for approximately 30–40 minutes until the muffins are well risen, golden and springy to touch. Remove from the oven and cool on a wire rack.

Once cool these muffins can be stored in an airtight container for 3 or 4 days, or can be frozen in plastic bags – just take one out of the freezer the evening before you want to enjoy it.

French toast is the perfect indulgence for a lazy Sunday morning, and it is especially good when it oozes with this delicious banana and nut filling. The berry compote adds a refreshingly fruity flavour but maple syrup is also good.

french toast stuffed with banana

2 eggs

50 ml/3 tablespoons milk

½ banana

freshly grated zest and freshly squeezed juice of ½ orange

a handful of almonds, pecans or walnuts, roughly chopped (optional)

¼ teaspoon ground allspice

2 slices white bread (slightly stale/dry or very lightly toasted in the oven)

½ tablespoon butter

salt and freshly ground black pepper

To serve

icing/confectioners' sugar (optional)

Berry Compote (page 12) or maple syrup, as preferred

Serves 1

Preheat the oven to 200°C (400°F) Gas 6.

Lightly beat the eggs, milk, and a little salt and pepper together in a small bowl. In a separate bowl, lightly crush the banana, then stir through the orange juice and zest, chopped nuts and allspice.

Spread the banana filling on 1 slice of bread, then top with the other slice to make a sandwich. Soak the sandwich in the egg mixture for 5–10 minutes, turning half way to make sure that both sides have absorbed the mixture.

Melt the butter in a frying pan/skillet set over medium heat. Put the sandwich into the pan and cook until brown on both sides. Finish in the preheated oven for 5–10 minutes to heat through to the centre. Remove the sandwich from the oven and slice on the diagonal. Dust liberally with icing/confectioners' sugar (if using) and serve with a spoonful of berry compote or maple syrup, as preferred.

This hearty breakfast quesadilla is a complete departure from traditional Mexican ingredients. If you want to make it more authentic, replace the baked beans with refried beans.

ham and egg breakfast quesadilla with baked beans

1 thick slice ham

2 large soft flour tortillas

50 g/¼ cup grated Cheddar or Monterey Jack cheese

200-g/7-oz. can baked beans in tomato sauce

1 teaspoon vegetable oil

1 tablespoon butter

1 large egg

salt and freshly ground black pepper

Serves 1

To assemble the quesadilla, place the ham on 1 of the tortillas. Sprinkle over the cheese and spoon on the beans. Use the back of the spoon to spread the beans to the edge of the tortilla. Top with the other tortilla and press down gently.

Heat the oil in a non-stick frying pan/skillet set over medium heat. When the oil is hot, carefully slide or lift the quesadilla into the pan, lower the heat and cook for 2–3 minutes, until the quesadilla is golden on one side and the cheese has begun to melt. Turn over (using a fish slice) and cook the other side for 2–3 minutes.

Meanwhile, melt the butter in a small non-stick frying pan/skillet. Add the egg and fry until cooked through, turning once to cook both sides if desired.

To serve, top the quesadilla with the fried egg and season with salt and pepper. Cut into wedges and eat immediately.

A hearty pork burger with all the traditional breakfast trimmings, perfect for the days when cereal just won't cut it.

big breakfast burger with a portobello mushroom and a fried egg

For the burgers

2 tablespoons olive oil

5 mushrooms, finely chopped

200 g/7 oz. lean minced/ground pork

2 teaspoons tomato ketchup

a pinch of mustard powder

3 tablespoons fresh breadcrumbs

salt and freshly ground black pepper

For 1 serving

1 English muffin

tomato ketchup

1 fried egg

1 grilled/broiled Portobello mushroom

Makes 2 burgers (one can be frozen for another time)

Heat 1 tablespoon of the oil in a frying pan/skillet set over medium heat. Add the chopped mushrooms and fry until soft and brown. Remove from the heat and set aside to cool.

Put the pork in a bowl with the tomato ketchup, mustard powder, breadcrumbs and salt and pepper. Work together with your hands until evenly mixed. Add the cooled mushrooms and mix again. Divide the mixture in half and shape into 2 burger patties. Press each burger down to make them nice and flat. To save one for another time, wrap and freeze it at this stage. Defrost thoroughly and cook as below.

Heat the remaining oil in the same frying pan/skillet and fry the burger over medium–high heat for 5 minutes on each side until cooked through.

Slice the English muffin in half and lightly toast it under the grill/broiler or in the toaster. Spread a spoonful of tomato ketchup on the base and put the cooked burger on top. Put a fried egg and a grilled/broiled Portobello mushroom on top and finish with the muffin lid. Serve with extra tomato ketchup on the side.

Garlicky mushrooms are great for breakfast, but try them on a layer of soft, creamy goat cheese and you will be in utter heaven. The kind of cheese you are looking for is a soft fresh cheese, not aged, so it will not have a rind. You could also use ricotta if you like. Seek out a good, sturdy rustic bread such as sourdough for this dish to prevent the underneath going soggy.

garlic mushrooms and goat cheese on sourdough toast

4 field mushrooms

2 small garlic cloves, crushed

2 tablespoons olive oil

1 tablespoon pine nuts

1 tablespoon balsamic vinegar

2 slices sourdough bread

75 g/2½ oz. fresh goat cheese

chopped tarragon, to serve

salt and freshly ground black pepper

Serves 1

Preheat the oven to 200°C (400°F) Gas 6.

Put the mushrooms, garlic and oil in a roasting pan. Toss well and season with salt and pepper. Roast in the preheated oven for 15 minutes, until tender. Stir in the pine nuts and balsamic vinegar halfway through roasting.

Just before the mushrooms are ready, toast the slices of sourdough bread and spread with the goat cheese. Place the mushrooms on top, stalk side up, scatter with the tarragon and serve immediately. Add more seasoning, if necessary.

Rostis make a fantastic brunch dish topped with a poached egg. They are equally good made with parsnips, carrots or beetroot, and can easily be doubled up and frozen ready for cooking for another time.

potato and celeriac rosti with spinach, mushrooms and a poached egg

100 g/3½ oz. potatoes, scrubbed and halved

100 g/3½ oz. celeriac/celery root, peeled and cut into large chunks

3 tablespoons olive oil

3–4 chestnut/cremini or 1 portobello mushroom, sliced

½ garlic clove, crushed

50 g/scant 1 cup baby spinach, washed, dried and finely chopped

1 egg, chilled

truffle oil, for drizzling (optional)

salt and freshly ground black pepper

Serves 1 generously

Preheat the oven to 180°C (350°F) Gas 4.

Bring a large pan of water to the boil and boil the potatoes for 6 minutes until they start to soften. Drain and cool. Bring another large pan of water to the boil and add the celeriac/celery root. Boil for 5 minutes until it starts to soften slightly. Drain and set aside to cool. Grate the potatoes and celeriac/celery root with a coarse grater, stir through 1 tablespoon of the oil and season well with salt and pepper.

Heat 1 tablespoon of the oil in a large frying pan/skillet set over medium–high heat. Put a large spoonful of the rosti mixture into the pan and flatten it down well to 1 cm/⅜ inch thick. Cook for 2–3 minutes on each side, until crisp and golden. Repeat until all the rosti mixture is used up – you may need to cook them in batches if there is not enough room in the pan. Transfer the fried rosti to the oven and bake for 5 minutes.

Meanwhile, heat the remaining oil in a separate frying pan/skillet. Add the mushrooms and garlic and cook over medium heat until golden. Season with salt and pepper and stir in the spinach to wilt.

When the rosti are ready, poach the egg, if using. Bring a pan of water to the boil, turn the heat down to a simmer and stir the water with a spoon to make a whirlpool. As the whirlpool dies, crack the egg into the centre of the pan. Cook for about 3 minutes, until the white is set but the yolk is still runny. Remove the egg from the pan with a slotted spoon and drain well. Put the rosti on a serving plate and top with the mushrooms, spinach, egg, a drizzle of truffle oil, if liked, and a generous grinding of black pepper. Serve immediately.

chapter 2

light bites

soups, salads and sandwiches

Puy lentils, grown in France, are great at thickening soups without turning sludgy. They give it a pert little bite, which is offset by the soft, buttery vegetables. Soups like this one are perfect for making in batches and freezing to eat later.

chunky puy lentil and vegetable soup

50 g/3½ tablespoons butter

2 carrots, peeled and finely chopped

2 leeks, white part only, thinly sliced

1 large onion, finely chopped

3 garlic cloves, sliced

½ teaspoon dried chilli/chile flakes

2 teaspoons dried oregano

400-g/14-oz. can chopped plum tomatoes

200 g/generous 1 cup Puy lentils

1 litre/4 cups vegetable stock

salt and freshly ground black pepper

crusty bread, toasted and buttered, to serve

finely grated pecorino or Parmesan cheese, to serve

Makes 4–6 servings (the rest can be frozen for another time)

Melt the butter in a large casserole dish or heavy-based saucepan. Add the carrots, leeks, onion and garlic and a large pinch of salt.

Stir until everything is coated in butter and cook over medium heat, with the lid on, for 15 minutes, stirring occasionally.

Once the vegetables have softened, add the chilli/chile flakes, oregano, tomatoes, lentils and stock. Cover again and leave to simmer for 30 minutes, or until the lentils are tender. Season with salt and freshly ground black pepper to taste.

Ladel into a serving bowl and enjoy with buttered toast and grated pecorino or Parmesan cheese on the side to sprinkle.

This is a cross between a soup and a risotto and should be soupy in consistency. Even when there's nothing else at hand you'll most likely have a bag of frozen peas in the freezer and some rice in the cupboard. The pancetta is optional but adds a nice salty note and any leftover could be added to the Minestrone recipe on page 32.

minty pea risotto soup

30 g/2 tablespoons butter

1 onion, finely chopped

150 g/1 cup cubed pancetta

400 g/3¼ cups frozen peas, defrosted, or fresh if available

2 tablespoons extra virgin olive oil, plus extra for drizzling

150 g/¾ cup risotto rice

1.5 litres/6 cups chicken or vegetable stock, plus extra if necessary

2 tablespoons shredded mint

salt and freshly ground black pepper

finely grated Parmesan cheese, to serve

a food processor

Makes 4 servings (the rest can be frozen for another time)

Melt the butter in a medium saucepan, then add the onion and pancetta. Cook over medium–low heat, with the lid on, for 8 minutes, or until the onion is softened and translucent. Stir occasionally.

Meanwhile, put half the peas in a food processor with the olive oil and blend until puréed.

Add the rice to the softened onion and stir until well coated in butter. Pour in the stock and add the puréed peas. Simmer, uncovered, for 15 minutes.

Add the remaining peas, season well and cook for a further 8–10 minutes, or until the rice is tender. Stir in the mint and add a little more stock if you think it needs to be soupier.

Transfer to a serving bowl, drizzle with olive oil and scatter with freshly ground black pepper. Serve with grated Parmesan cheese.

This is a filling soup made more substantial with the addition of beans and pasta. It will keep in the fridge for two days, where the flavours will develop and thicken slightly.

minestrone

140 g/⅔ cup dried haricot or cannellini beans

2 tablespoons olive or vegetable oil

1 large onion, finely diced

2 celery stalks, finely diced

1 large carrot, finely diced

1 teaspoon dried thyme

3–5 garlic cloves, thinly sliced

250 ml/1 cup red or white wine

1.5 litres/6 cups chicken or vegetable stock

225 g/8 oz. canned chopped tomatoes

1 small courgette/zucchini, diced

100 g/⅔ cup green beans, diced

50 g/½ cup small dried pasta or broken spaghetti

1 teaspoon sea salt

freshly ground black pepper

1 teaspoon sugar (optional)

a large handful each of chopped flat-leaf parsley and basil

finely grated Parmesan cheese, to serve

Makes 6 servings (the rest can be frozen for another time)

Put the haricot or cannellini beans in a bowl, cover with cold water and leave to soak overnight. The next day, discard the soaking water and transfer the beans to a saucepan. Re-cover the beans with fresh water and place the pan over high heat. Bring to the boil, remove any froth that rises to the surface and boil gently for 1–1½ hours, until the beans are tender. Leave to cool, then drain and discard the water.

Heat the oil in a large saucepan, add the onion, celery and carrot and cook for 5–10 minutes until softened and well coloured, taking care not to burn them. Stir in the thyme, garlic and wine and bring to the boil. Boil for 1 minute to cook off the alcohol.

Stir in the stock, tomatoes and cooked beans. Bring to the boil, then reduce the heat to simmer. Cover with the lid and cook for 40–50 minutes.

Add the courgette/zucchini, green beans and pasta and cook for a further 15 minutes until the vegetables and pasta are tender. Taste and season with salt and black pepper. Add sugar to taste if the tomatoes make the soup too acidic.

Stir in the fresh herbs and ladle into a warmed soup bowl. Top with grated Parmesan and freshly ground black pepper and eat immediately.

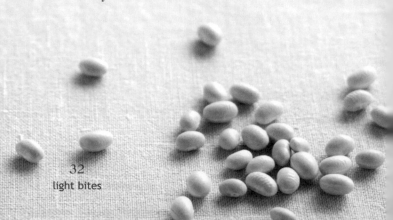

Pomegranate molasses is a thick, sticky liquid made from reduced pomegranate juice and used in Middle Eastern cooking. You can buy it from Middle Eastern grocers or some 'special selection' sections of supermarkets. It instantly lifts the flavour of summer fruits, duck breasts and chicken, and is a well-kept secret of many professional kitchens. If you can't get hold of pomegranate molasses, use a good, thick, syrupy balsamic vinegar or reduce a thinner vinegar slowly in a small pan until it has halved in volume.

beetroot, walnut and warm goat cheese salad

1 tablespoon pomegranate molasses or balsamic vinegar

½ tablespoon walnut oil

freshly squeezed juice of ½ orange

½ garlic clove, crushed

100 g/3½ oz. cooked fresh beetroot/beet (not pickled), quartered

2 thick slices ciabatta bread

50 g/scant ½ cup crumbled firm goat cheese

50 g/2 oz. mixed salad leaves/greens

25 g/¼ cup walnut halves

Serves 1

To make the dressing, mix together the pomegranate molasses or balsamic vinegar, walnut oil, orange juice and garlic in a small bowl. Put the quartered beetroot/beets in a non-metallic bowl and pour the dressing over the top. Cover with clingfilm/plastic wrap and leave to marinate in a cool place for about 20 minutes.

Meanwhile, preheat the grill/broiler to medium and lightly toast one side of the ciabatta bread. Turn the bread over and arrange the goat cheese on the other side. Grill/broil for a further 3–4 minutes, or until the top begins to turn golden.

Arrange the salad leaves/greens and walnuts on a serving plate, top with the marinated beetroot/beet and goat cheese toasts and pour over the remaining dressing.

This combination of baby spinach, crunchy croûtes, blue cheese, grapes and pears is a sensation. Look out for the traditional French bread called ficelle, which has a hard, dark brown crust and many large air pockets. It makes delicious toasts, but if you can't find it, Italian ciabatta is more readily available and works well.

pear, blue cheese and croûte salad

For the croûtes

50 g/2 oz. ficelle French bread or ciabatta

1 tablespoon extra virgin olive oil

a few rosemary and thyme sprigs

salt and freshly ground black pepper

For the salad

1 tablespoon Sweet Mustard Dressing (page 45)

a handful of baby spinach leaves

25 g/¼ cup crumbled Roquefort, Stilton or other firm blue cheese

about 8 red seedless grapes, halved

½ ripe pear, cored and sliced

Serves 1

Preheat the oven to 200°F (400°C) Gas 6.

First make the croûtes. Cut the bread into thin slices and place them on a baking sheet. Drizzle with the olive oil and sprinkle with salt and pepper to taste, and with the rosemary and thyme sprigs.

Place the baking sheet in the preheated oven and cook the croûtes for about 10 minutes, or until the bread is toasted.

Pour the mustard dressing into a large bowl, add the spinach, cheese, grapes and pear and toss lightly. Pile the dressed salad into a serving bowl and top with the croûtes.

You can keep any leftover crunchy croûtes in an airtight container for up to 2 weeks. Simply refresh them in a warm oven before eating. Enjoy them with other salads or simply spread them with soft cheese, houmous or pâté as a snack.

It's best to use the crunchiest leaves in this salad, but you could, for a change, add some peppery wild rocket leaves or salad leaves left over from another dish. The salmon has been coated in a ready-made Cajun seasoning, found in the spice section of most supermarkets.

blackened salmon salad

1 garlic clove, halved

2 tablespoons olive oil

1 thick slice ciabatta bread, cut into cubes

1 tablespoon Cajun seasoning

½ teaspoon flaky sea salt

1 skinless salmon fillet (weighing about 150 g/5 oz.)

1 Little Gem/Bibb lettuce or ½ Cos lettuce, shredded

Parmesan cheese shavings, to serve

For the dressing

½ garlic clove, crushed

100 ml/scant ½ cup mayonnaise

2 anchovy fillets, finely chopped

freshly ground black pepper

a small food processor or blender

Serves 1

Put the garlic clove halves in a heavy-based frying pan/skillet with 1 tablespoon of the olive oil. Heat, then add the bread cubes. Toast over medium heat, tossing frequently, until the cubes are evenly golden brown. Tip them onto paper towel, discard the garlic and set aside. Wipe the pan clean.

Meanwhile, to make the dressing, put the crushed garlic in the bowl of a food processor or blender along with the mayonnaise and anchovy fillets and process until smooth. Add a few drops of hot water to thin the dressing so that it is the consistency of double/heavy cream. Season to taste with black pepper.

Mix together the Cajun seasoning and salt on a plate and roll the salmon fillets in the seasoning mix until evenly covered. Place the clean frying pan/skillet over high heat and add the remaining oil. When the pan is smoking, add the salmon and cook for 2–3 minutes on each side, until just cooked. Remove from the heat and break into rough pieces.

Pour the dressing into a large bowl. Add the shredded lettuce and toss well to coat. Arrange the dressed lettuce on a serving plate. Top with the blackened salmon pieces, garlic croutons and a sprinkling of Parmesan shavings. Eat immediately.

This unusual and delicious Thai-style chicken salad makes great use of a rotisserie-cooked chicken picked up on your way home from work. The leftovers will be great in a lunchbox or with steamed rice for dinner the next day, or halve the salad quantities and see pages 74 and 76 for other ways to use the rest of the chicken.

coconut thai chicken salad

900-g/2-lb. rotisserie-cooked chicken, preferably still warm

200 ml/scant 1 cup canned coconut milk

2 tablespoons sweet chilli/chile dipping sauce

4 teaspoons fish sauce

freshly squeezed juice of 1 lime

1 carrot, peeled and cut into sticks

50 g/3–4 radishes, thinly sliced

1 red bell pepper, deseeded and thinly sliced

3 spring onions/scallions, thinly sliced

1 Cos lettuce, torn into bite-sized pieces

2 tablespoons roasted peanuts or cashew nuts, roughly chopped

a handful of mint leaves

1 lime, quartered

Makes 2–4 servings

Remove the flesh from the roast chicken carcass, including the wings and the legs. Tear the flesh into bite-size pieces.

Pour the coconut milk, sweet chilli/chile sauce, fish sauce and lime juice into a bowl and mix well using a fork. Add the chicken meat to the bowl and toss it gently in the coconut dressing until coated.

Put the carrot, radishes, red (bell) peppers, spring onions/ scallions and lettuce in a bowl and toss to mix, then place the mixture on a serving plate. Arrange the coconut chicken pieces on top and spoon any remaining dressing over the top.

Sprinkle the salad with the chopped peanuts or cashew nuts, garnish with mint leaves and squeeze the lime quarters over it. Eat immediately.

Variation: If you want to make the salad more substantial, you can add rice noodles. Place 150 g/5 oz. rice noodles in a large heatproof bowl, cover with boiling water and leave to sit for 3–5 minutes until just tender before draining in a colander. Toss these with the chicken and coconut dressing and serve on top of the salad.

Peppermint tea is great for fluffing up the grains of couscous, and works well alongside the sweet squash and salty, squeaky halloumi. Leftover halloumi can be enjoyed in the recipes on pages 53 and 72.

mint tea couscous with roast squash, halloumi, dates and pistachios

100 g/3½ oz. butternut squash or pumpkin, peeled, deseeded and cut into wedges

1 tablespoon extra virgin olive oil

1 bay leaf

1 sprig thyme

1 unpeeled garlic clove

½ large dried chilli/chile

125 g/4 oz. halloumi cheese, cubed

a handful of pistachios, shelled and chopped

1 peppermint tea bag

50 g/¼ cup couscous

30 g/scant ¼ cup fresh Medjool dates, pitted and finely chopped

½ tablespoon extra virgin olive oil

salt and freshly ground black pepper

Serves 1

Preheat the oven to 200°C (400°F) Gas 6.

Put the squash in a roasting pan, drizzle with a little of the olive oil and tuck in the bay leaf, thyme, garlic and chilli/chile. Roast in the preheated oven for 25 minutes, or until the squash is almost tender. Raise the oven temperature to 240°C (475°F) Gas 9. Add the halloumi and pistachios to the roasting pan, drizzle with the remaining olive oil and roast for a further 10 minutes, or until the halloumi is golden.

Meanwhile, put the peppermint tea bag in a heatproof jug/pitcher or a teapot and pour over 75 ml/⅓ cup just-boiled water. Leave to steep for 1 minute, then discard the tea bag. Put the couscous and dates in a large bowl, season to taste and pour over the hot tea. Cover with clingfilm/plastic wrap and leave for 5 minutes, or until the grains have swollen and absorbed all the tea.

Fluff up the couscous with a fork, stirring in about half the ingredients from the roasting pan at the same time, but leaving behind the chilli/chile. Spoon into a serving bowl and top with the remaining ingredients. Drizzle with a little olive oil and eat immediately.

A good salad dressing is only as good as the ingredients you use. For simple salad leaves, combine extra virgin olive oil, a drop of balsamic vinegar and a sprinkling of sea salt and freshly ground black pepper in a salad bowl before you add the salad leaves. Or try these dressings, which keep well in a jar in the fridge for 1 week. Always shake well before use.

salad dressings

caesar dressing

This is a speedy version of the popular dressing. It's perfect with any green salad leaves/greens and works well with roast chicken or avocado.

1 very fresh free-range egg
1 garlic clove, crushed
2 teaspoons Worcestershire sauce
1 teaspoon anchovy essence
1 tablespoon freshly squeezed lime juice
3 tablespoons extra virgin olive oil
25 g/1 oz. Parmesan cheese, freshly grated
freshly ground black pepper

Put the egg in a pan of cold water and bring to the boil. Boil for 1 minute, then plunge it into cold water to stop the cooking process. Once the egg is cool enough to handle, crack it into a mini food processor and add the garlic, Worcestershire sauce, anchovy essence, lime juice and olive oil. Process well, then stir in the Parmesan cheese and add pepper to taste.

blue cheese dressing

This is a great dressing for using up those leftover bits of blue cheese lurking in the back of your fridge. Blue cheese goes particularly well with pears, or can be used to liven up a chicken salad.

50 g/2 oz. firm blue cheese, such as Stilton or Roquefort
2 tablespoons sherry or cider vinegar
3 tablespoons walnut or hazelnut oil
3 tablespoons sunflower oil
1 teaspoon Worcestershire sauce
freshly squeezed lemon juice, to taste
freshly ground black pepper

Put all the ingredients, except the lemon juice, in the bowl of a food processor and process until smooth. Add a little lemon juice and pepper to taste.

sweet mustard dressing

This dressing is slightly sweeter than a classic vinaigrette. It has a creamy emulsified texture and is good for drizzling over sliced tomatoes and mozzarella, or works well with bitter salad leaves like chicory/endive, rocket/arugula or frisée lettuce. If you prefer, you could use American-style yellow mustard instead of Dijon.

1 tablespoon Dijon mustard

2 teaspoons acacia or lavender honey

1 tablespoon cider vinegar

6 tablespoons extra virgin olive oil

salt and freshly ground black pepper

Put all the ingredients in a screw-top jar and shake vigorously until the dressing is emulsified. Add salt and pepper to taste.

herb vinaigrette

The sprigs of herbs and garlic used here will infuse more into the vinaigrette the longer they are left in the dressing. It is the most useful and versatile dressing in the kitchen.

1 tablespoon freshly squeezed lemon juice

1 tablespoon white wine vinegar or tarragon vinegar

1 teaspoon caster/granulated sugar

100 ml/½ cup extra virgin olive oil

1 garlic clove, halved

a few herb sprigs, such as tarragon, coriander/cilantro or mint

salt and freshly ground black pepper

Put the lemon juice, vinegar, sugar and olive oil in a screw-top jar. Shake the jar vigorously until the dressing is smooth. Add the garlic halves and herb sprigs and season with salt and pepper to taste.

garlic and saffron aioli

This is delicious served with grilled/broiled or barbecued fish or chicken, or served as a dip for potato wedges. Look out for smoked garlic – it has a much less intense flavour.

150 ml/⅔ cup good-quality mayonnaise

2 garlic cloves, crushed

a pinch of cayenne pepper

a pinch of saffron threads

1 tablespoon extra virgin olive oil

Put the ingredients in a bowl and whisk to combine. Cover with clingfilm/plastic wrap and chill in the fridge for about 1–2 hours, to allow the flavour to develop fully. Stir well.

mediterranean salsa

This is perfect for cheering up grilled/broiled or barbecued fish fillets or chicken breasts, or serving as a dip. A spoonful will also brighten up a ready-made soup.

1 tablespoon red wine vinegar

2 tablespoons small capers, rinsed, drained and finely chopped

1 garlic clove, crushed

½ teaspoon anchovy essence

½ teaspoon Dijon mustard

2 tablespoons chopped mixed herbs, such as basil, tarragon, parsley and mint

freshly squeezed juice of ½ lemon

½ small onion, finely chopped

150 ml/⅔ cup extra virgin olive oil

freshly ground black pepper

Put the vinegar, capers, garlic, anchovy essence and mustard in a heavy-based bowl and use the end of a rolling pin to work the mixture until evenly combined. Whisk in the herbs, lemon juice, onion, olive oil and pepper, to taste.

This is fantastic as a quick-fix supper – and if you're short of time, buy a tub of good-quality ready-made potato salad and mix it with half the amount of the dill dressing. The Smoked Trout Hash on page 63 is a great way of using up any unused smoked trout.

smoked trout, warm new potato and beetroot salad

75 g/⅔ cup small new potatoes, halved if larger

75 g/2½ oz. smoked trout fillets, skinned and flaked

1 cooked fresh beetroot/beet (not pickled), sliced into wedges

½ head chicory/Belgian endive, thickly sliced

For the dill dressing

½ teaspoon wholegrain mustard

½ tablespoon beer or lager

½ teaspoon caster/granulated sugar

1 tablespoon extra virgin olive oil

1 tablespoon chopped dill, plus extra sprigs to garnish

salt and freshly ground black pepper

Serves 1

Put the new potatoes in a large pan, add sufficient cold water to cover, add a little salt and bring to the boil. Cook for 10–15 minutes, until just tender.

Meanwhile, make the dressing. Put the mustard, beer or lager, sugar, olive oil and chopped dill in a small bowl and use a small whisk or fork to combine. Season to taste with salt and freshly ground black pepper.

Drain the potatoes and, when cool enough to handle, slice thickly and put in a bowl with half of the dressing. Toss to coat.

Arrange the trout fillet flakes, slices of warm dressed potato, beetroot/beet wedges and chicory on a serving plate and garnish with the sprigs of dill. Drizzle the remaining dressing over the top and eat immediately.

sangria prawn salad

350 g/¾ lb fresh shell-on prawns/shrimp (or 175 g/6 oz. shelled prawns/shrimp)

½ orange

½ teaspoon sugar (optional)

125 ml/½ cup fruity red wine

80 ml/⅓ cup olive oil

freshly grated zest of ¼ lemon

3 garlic cloves (2 thinly sliced, 1 crushed)

¼ red chilli/chile, diced

¼ small green apple, diced

a small handful of mint, roughly chopped

salt and freshly ground black pepper

crusty bread, to serve

Serves 1

Preheat the oven to 200°C (400°F) Gas 6.

Prepare the prawns/shrimp by removing the heads and peeling off the shell and legs. Keep the tails on if you like but remove if preferred. Slit the backs with a knife and lift out the the black vein. Put them in a baking dish, cover and set aside.

Using a vegetable peeler, make 2 long strips of orange zest. Put the strips of zest in a small saucepan and add the red wine. Heat over high heat and cook until reduced by two-thirds and syrupy. Taste and if it's too sharp add the sugar.

Pour the olive oil over the prawns/shrimp in the baking dish. Grate in the remaining orange and lemon zests. Add the garlic and chilli/chile. Cover the dish with foil and cook in the preheated oven for about 15–18 minutes, until pink (the larger the prawns/shrimp, the longer they will take to cook).

Transfer the prawns/shrimp to a shallow serving bowl, drizzle with the red wine syrup and top with diced apple and chopped mint. Season to taste with salt and pepper. Serve with crusty bread on the side to mop up the fruity juices.

gravadlax and pickled cucumber open sandwich

100 g/3½ oz. cucumber

1 teaspoon white wine vinegar

½ teaspoon chopped dill

1 slice light rye or Irish soda bread

1 tablespoon crème fraîche

50 g/2 oz. gravadlax

freshly ground black pepper (or mixed peppercorns)

Serves 1

Peel the cucumber and halve it lengthways. Scoop out the seeds using a teaspoon and cut it into wafer-thin, crescent-shaped slices. Pat these dry with paper towels and put them in a large bowl.

Put the vinegar and chopped dill in a small bowl, season with a little freshly ground black pepper (or mixed peppercorns) and use a fork to combine. Pour the dressing over the cucumber and toss to coat.

Lightly toast the bread and, while it's still warm, spread generously with crème fraîche. Top with the marinated cucumber salad and slices of gravadlax. Eat immediately.

What elevates this grilled cheese sandwich above the crowd is carefully choosing the right blend of cheese: mozzarella for its melting quality, something intense like a good strong Cheddar and Swiss cheese for a hint of nuttiness. Perfect enjoyed as a substantial snack or late night supper, alongside a cup of your favourite tomato soup.

ultimate three-cheese toastie

butter, softened

2 large slices white bread

35 g/⅓ cup grated Lincolnshire Poacher or mature/sharp Cheddar cheese

65 g/2½ oz. soft mozzarella cheese, sliced

35 g/⅓ cup grated Emmental/Swiss cheese

a cup of tomato soup, to serve (optional)

Serves 1

Butter the bread slices on one side each.

Without turning the heat on, place one slice of bread in a large, non-stick frying pan/skillet, butter-side down. Sprinkle the bread in the pan with the grated/shredded Lincolnshire Poacher or Cheddar in an even layer. Top with the mozzarella slices, then sprinkle the grated/shredded Emmental/Swiss cheese on top. Finally, enclose with the remaining bread slice, butter-side up.

Turn on the heat to medium and cook the first side for 3–5 minutes, until it turns a deep golden colour. Carefully turn with a spatula and cook on the second side for 2–3 minutes, or until deep golden brown all over.

Remove from the frying pan/skillet, transfer to a plate and cut the sandwich into quarters. Let cool for a few minutes before serving with hot tomato soup, if liked.

Halloumi is a very salty Cypriot cheese which takes well to grilling/broiling since it does not melt if kept in slices. It's served here with ready-made falafel and a tahini (sesame seed) sauce so it's a healthy and nutritious light meal, as well as a delicious one.

hot halloumi and falafel wrap with tahini sauce

1 flatbread or sandwich wrap

extra virgin olive oil, for frying and brushing

4 slices halloumi cheese, about 5 mm/¼ inch thick

plain/all-purpose flour, lightly seasoned, for dusting

1 cooked beetroot/beet (about 60 g/2½ oz.), thinly sliced

3–4 ready-made falafel, warmed in a low oven as per the package instructions

lemon wedges, to serve

For the tahini sauce

40 g/scant /¼ cup tahini

freshly squeezed juice of ¼ lemon, plus extra to taste

salt and freshly ground black pepper

Serves 1

For the sauce, combine the tahini and lemon juice and just enough water to obtain a nice dipping sauce consistency. Taste and adjust the seasoning and add more lemon juice if required. Set aside.

Rub a little olive oil over a ridged griddle/grill pan and set over medium heat. Dust the halloumi slices in seasoned flour and add them to the pan. Grill for just 1 or 2 minutes on each side and turn using metal tongs. Remove from the pan and put on a plate until needed. Brush the outside of the flatbread with a little oil and arrange oil-side down on a clean work surface or chopping/cutting board. Arrange the grilled halloumi slices down one side, add a layer of beetroot/beet slices on top (use all of it up) and follow with the falafel, which should be gently pressed with the back of a fork to allow them to spread out over the sandwich. Carefully fold the empty flatbread half over the top of the filled half to form a canopy.

Place the sandwich in the pan. Turn the heat to medium and cook 3–4 minutes on the first side. Carefully turn with a large spatula and cook on the second side for 2–3 minutes more, pressing down gently on this side until golden brown all over.

Remove from the pan and cut in half. Let cool for a few minutes before eating with the tahini sauce for dipping and a couple of lemon wedges for squeezing.

This has all the taste elements of a Friday night Indian takeaway but in one satisfying portion. Choose a good mango chutney, something with a hint of spicy ginger as it partners the melted paneer amazingly well. Some cucumber and mint raita, in a small dish, makes the perfect cooling dip.

tandoori chicken and paneer stuffed naan with mango chutney

1 boneless, skinless chicken breast (about 150 g/5 oz.)

2–3 tablespoons tandoori paste

butter, softened, for spreading

1 naan bread

2–3 tablespoons mango chutney, plus extra to serve

1 thin slice mild cheese, such as Gouda or Fontina

50 g/⅓ cup grated paneer cheese

salt

For the raita dip

¼ cucumber, finely chopped

125 ml/generous ½ cup plain yogurt

a small handful of mint, chopped

a large pinch of salt

Serves 1

Preheat the oven to 180°C (350°F) Gas 4. Coat the chicken with the tandoori paste, season lightly with salt and bake until cooked through, about 20–25 minutes. Let cool, then slice thinly.

While the chicken is cooking, prepare the raita dip by squeezing any excess moisture from the cucumber with paper towels, then mixing together all of the ingredients thoroughly. Set aside. Butter the naan bread on one side and set aside.

This is easiest if assembled in a large heavy-based non-stick frying pan/skillet. Butter the naan bread on one side and put it in the pan/skillet, butter-side down. You will need to fold the bread over to form a sandwich, so position the filling on one side. Put one slice of cheese on the naan, then arrange the chicken slices over the top. Drop spoonfuls of the chutney on top, then spread the spoonfuls out, gently and evenly, with the back of a spoon. Sprinkle with the paneer. Fold the other half of the bread over the top to cover.

Turn the heat to medium and cook the first side for 3–5 minutes until deep golden, pressing down gently with a spatula. Carefully turn with a large spatula and cook on the second side for 2–3 minutes more, or until deep golden brown all over.

Remove from the pan/skillet and transfer to a plate. Let cool for a few minutes before eating with the raita dip and some extra mango chutney.

chapter 3

fast food

quick and easy weeknight dishes

tagliatelle with peas and goat cheese pesto

50 g/⅓ cup frozen peas

100 g/3½ oz. tagliatelle

finely grated Parmesan cheese, to serve

For the pesto

½ small garlic clove

½ large green chilli/chile, deseeded

10 g/½ oz. basil leaves, plus extra to serve

1 tablespoon pine nuts

1½ tablespoons extra virgin olive oil

25 g/1 oz. goat cheese

salt and freshly ground black pepper

an electric blender or mortar and pestle

Serves 1

To make the pesto, put the garlic, chilli/chile, basil and a large pinch of salt in a food processor and process until roughly chopped. Alternatively, crush everything with a pestle and mortar.

Put the pine nuts in a dry frying pan/skillet and toast over low heat for a few minutes, shaking the pan, until golden all over. Add them to the pesto and process again until coarsely chopped. Add half the olive oil and process again. Stir in the remaining oil and the crumbled goat cheese. Taste and season.

Bring a large pan of salted water and a small pan of unsalted water to the boil. Add the peas to the smaller pan and simmer for about 3 minutes. Cook the tagliatelle in the large pan according to the packet instructions, until it is al dente. Drain and return to the pan. Add a dollop of pesto and the peas to the tagliatelle and toss them through, then add the remaining pesto, making sure all the pasta is thoroughly coated. Sprinkle with basil and Parmesan to serve.

tagliatelle with broccoli, anchovy, parmesan and crème fraîche

100 g/3½ oz. tagliatelle

150 g/2 heaped cups broccoli florets

1 tablespoon olive oil

¼ teaspoon dried chilli/chile flakes

1 garlic clove, crushed

1 anchovy fillet, roughly chopped

50 g/2 oz. crème fraîche

salt and freshly ground black pepper

finely grated Parmesan cheese, to serve

Serves 1

Bring a large pan of salted water to the boil. Add the tagliatelle and cook according to the packet instructions until al dente. Add the broccoli to the pasta 3–4 minutes before the end of cooking. Drain the pasta and the broccoli well, reserving a little of the cooking water.

Wipe out the pan and add the olive oil. Cook the garlic, chilli/chile flakes and anchovy over low heat for about 2 minutes. Add the crème fraîche, season with a little pepper and bring to the boil. Return the cooked broccoli and pasta to the pan, adding a little of the reserved pasta cooking water if necessary to thin the sauce down. Season with black pepper.

Transfer the pasta to a serving bowl and eat immediately, sprinkled with Parmesan cheese.

As far as real fast food goes, a bowl of deli pasta ticks all the boxes. Keep your fridge well stocked with a few key deli ingredients and a sustaining and comforting meal is never far from your table (or lap!). Buy good-quality dried pasta in a variety of shapes and sizes. The only fresh pastas worth buying for everyday eating are the filled varieties, such as ravioli or tortellini. Always keep a block of fresh Parmesan cheese to hand for grating over your chosen pasta dish.

deli pasta

pappardelle with artichoke hearts and parma ham

This is a quick and simple midweek supper that uses a tub of crème fraîche and some great deli ingredients to create a luxurious pasta dish that even non-cooks can make. If you can't find pappardelle, it will work just as well with tagliatelle.

125 g/4 oz. pappardelle (thick ribbons of pasta)

125 ml/scant ½ cup crème fraîche

1 garlic clove, crushed

1 teaspoon Dijon mustard

60 g/2½ oz. roasted and marinated artichoke hearts, drained and cut into small pieces

3 slices Parma ham, cut into strips

salt and freshly ground black pepper

freshly grated Parmesan cheese, to serve

Serves 1

Bring a large pan of salted water to the boil. Add the pasta and cook according to the packet instructions, until al dente. When it is ready, tip into a colander and drain well, reserving a little of the cooking water.

Add the crème fraîche, garlic and mustard to the pan and bring to a simmer. Add the cooked pasta, artichokes and Parma ham and stir everything together, thinning with a little of the reserved pasta cooking water if necessary. Season to taste with pepper.

Spoon the pasta into a warmed serving bowl and sprinkle with Parmesan cheese. Eat immediately.

more quick deli pasta ideas:

• *Spicy tomato fusilli* – sunblush tomatoes, crushed garlic, finely chopped red chilli/chile, shredded basil and chilli/chile oil or extra virgin olive oil, tossed through cooked fusilli pasta.

• *Creamy salmon and pea linguine* – hot smoked salmon flakes, salmon roe, cooked petit pois, finely chopped dill and crème fraîche, stirred into cooked linguine pasta.

• *Sweet pepper and anchovy penne* – Spanish-style chargrilled red bell peppers, chopped marinated anchovies, chilli/chile flakes and chopped flat-leaf parsley, added to cooked penne pasta.

• *Creamy bacon and mushroom spaghetti* – bacon lardons, chopped marinated wild mushrooms, crushed smoked garlic and crème fraîche, with cooked spaghetti.

• *Ricotta and spinach penne* – crumbled ricotta cheese, sliced black olives, baby spinach leaves and a drizzle of extra virgin olive oil, tossed through cooked penne pasta.

A perfect supper dish that's speedy to make and satisfying to eat. You could serve it with crusty bread and a peppery watercress salad, and any leftovers would make a lovely lunchbox the next day. The salad on page 47 is a great way to use up any leftover smoked trout.

smoked trout hash with horseradish cream

250 g/1½ cups baby new potatoes, scrubbed

1 tablespoon butter

1–2 tablespoons olive oil

½ small red onion, finely chopped

½ celery stick/rib, finely chopped

¼ teaspoon paprika

½ tablespoon chopped dill

½ teaspoon finely grated lemon zest

125 g/4½ oz. smoked trout, cut into pieces

salt and freshly ground black pepper

lemon wedges, to serve

For the horseradish cream

2–3 tablespoons sour cream or Greek-style plain yogurt

1 teaspoon creamed horseradish

½ small bunch of chives, snipped

Serves 1

Put the potatoes in a large saucepan with enough water to cover. Add a pinch of salt and boil until tender when pierced with a knife. Drain. When cool enough to handle, cut into cubes.

Meanwhile, make the horseradish cream. Combine the sour cream, horseradish and chives in a small bowl. Mix, cover and set aside.

Melt the butter and 1 tablespoon of the oil in a large frying pan. Add the cubed potatoes with a pinch of salt and cook, stirring occasionally, for about 10 minutes, until browned.

Add the onion, celery, paprika, dill and lemon zest to the pan and cook, stirring occasionally, for 5 minutes more. Stir in the trout, season, and add a little more oil if the mixture seems dry. Continue cooking, turning every so often, until the hash is well browned.

Serve immediately with the horseradish cream and lemon wedges.

Variation: Replace the smoked trout with chopped bacon or ham, omit the lemon zest and use parsley in place of the dill. For a vegetarian version, replace the bacon with diced green bell pepper. Serve either variation with a fried egg on top, and a dash of Tabasco can replace the horseradish.

This is a great way to transform storecupboard staples or some leftover cooked rice into a luxurious feast with the addition of a few fresh ingredients. If you're really looking to spoil yourself, use freshly picked white crabmeat, but go easy on the flavourings, as you don't want to overwhelm the delicate sweetness of the crab.

wok-tossed jasmine rice with crabmeat and asparagus

1 tablespoon groundnut/peanut oil

½ small onion, finely chopped

1 garlic clove, crushed

½ large red chilli/chile, deseeded and finely chopped

60 g/2½ oz. fine asparagus, cut into 2-cm/¾-inch lengths, stalks and tips kept separately

½ tablespoon light soy sauce, plus extra if needed

100 g/scant ½ cup canned or fresh white crabmeat, well drained

125 g/1 cup cold, cooked jasmine rice

½ tablespoon sweet chilli/chile sauce

a dash of toasted sesame oil

1 tablespoon finely chopped chives

Serves 1

Heat the groundnut/peanut oil in a wok or large frying pan/skillet until hot. Add the onion and stir-fry over high heat for 2–3 minutes, or until softened and golden. Add the garlic and chilli/chile and cook for a further minute. Throw in the asparagus stalks and stir-fry for 2 minutes. Add the asparagus tips and 1 teaspoon of the soy sauce and stir-fry for 30 seconds. Stir in the crabmeat and cook over medium heat until heated through.

Mix in the rice, then pour in the chilli/chile sauce, sesame oil and remaining soy sauce. Stir well until everything is thoroughly combined and the rice is piping hot. Taste and add more soy sauce if you think it needs it, then stir in the chives and remove from the heat. Transfer to a deep bowl and eat immediately.

A plate of fried rice makes a lovely all-in-one meal, but it can get a little boring, especially if you stick to the same old formula. Ring the changes, without any extra fuss, by adding some green curry paste and coconut cream for a Thai twist.

green curry fried rice with chicken, green beans and peas

1–2 skinless and boneless chicken thighs, cut into 2-cm/ ¾-inch pieces

½ tablespoon fish sauce, plus extra to taste

¼ teaspoon finely grated fresh ginger

½ tablespoon vegetable oil

1 shallot, finely chopped

1 small garlic clove, crushed

1 tablespoon Thai green curry paste

1 tablespoon coconut cream

a handful of trimmed fine green beans, cut into 1-cm/½-inch lengths

a handful of frozen peas

100 g/¾ cup cold, cooked jasmine rice

leaves from a few sprigs of coriander/ cilantro, chopped

salt and freshly ground black pepper

thinly sliced fresh red chilli/chile, to garnish (optional)

a lime wedge, to serve

Serves 1

Put the chicken, half the fish sauce, the ginger and a little black pepper in a bowl and toss until well mixed.

Heat the oil in a wok or large frying pan/skillet until hot, add the shallot and stir-fry over high heat for 2–3 minutes, or until softened and golden. Add the garlic and cook for 1 minute. Stir in the curry paste, then after 1 minute stir in the coconut cream. Cook over high heat for 2–3 minutes until the cream has reduced by half.

Add the chicken and stir-fry over high heat for 3–4 minutes, or until sealed on the outside. Add the green beans and stir-fry for 2 minutes. Throw in the peas and cook for a further minute, until the vegetables are tender but still crunchy and the chicken is cooked through. Season with the remaining fish sauce.

Mix in the rice and stir over the heat until everything is well combined and the rice is piping hot. Season with salt or more fish sauce if you think it needs it, and stir in the chopped coriander/cilantro. Transfer to a deep serving bowl and garnish with chilli/chile, if using. Serve immediately with a lime wedge for squeezing.

As you need to marinate the chicken in the spices for 48 hours, this is a useful recipe to have up your sleeve for when you have bought a pack of two chicken breasts and used the first for another recipe, such as the Tandoori Chicken and Paneer Stuffed Naan with Mango Chutney on page 54.

chicken tandoori kebabs

1 skinless chicken breasts, cut into 6 bite-size pieces

½ tablespoon butter, melted

For the marinade

1 small fresh red or green chilli/chile, deseeded and chopped

1 small garlic clove, chopped

1 teaspoon finely chopped fresh ginger

½ tablespoon double/heavy cream or yogurt

1 tablespoon vegetable oil

¼ tablespoon paprika

½ teaspoon ground cumin

½ teaspoon ground cardamom

¼ teaspoon ground cloves

¼ teaspoon sea salt

To serve (optional)

crispy poppadoms

tomato and cucumber salad

lime wedges

2 metal skewers

an electric blender or mortar and pestle

Serves 1

To prepare the marinade, use a mortar and pestle, or an electric blender, to mince the chilli/chile, garlic and ginger to a paste. Beat in the cream and oil with 1–2 tablespoons water to form a smooth mixture. Beat in the dried spices.

Put the chicken pieces in a bowl and rub with the marinade until thoroughly coated. Cover with clingfilm/plastic wrap and chill in the fridge for about 48 hours. When you are ready to cook them, lift the chicken pieces out of the marinade and thread them onto the skewers. Preheat your grill/broiler to high. Brush the chicken with the melted butter and cook for 4–5 minutes, turning halfway through cooking, until the chicken is cooked through.

Enjoy with crispy poppadoms, a salad of finely diced tomato, cucumber and onion with fresh coriander/cilantro, and wedges of lime for squeezing, if liked.

Chermoula is a Moroccan spice rub often used for grilled dishes.
This recipe will make more chermoula than you need but store it in the
fridge in a sealed jar and use it as a marinade for lamb chops or
chicken, or mix it with mayonnaise or yogurt to make a tasty dip.

monkfish kebabs with chermoula

200 g/7 oz. monkfish tail or
skinless, boneless cod fillet,
cut into large chunks

4 cherry tomatoes

½ teaspoon smoked paprika

½ lemon, cut into wedges

cooked rice, to serve

For the chermoula

2 garlic cloves

1 teaspoon coarse sea salt

1–2 teaspoons cumin seeds,
crushed or ground

1 fresh red chilli/chile, deseeded
and chopped

freshly squeezed juice of 1 lemon

2 tablespoons olive oil

a small bunch of coriander/
cilantro, roughly chopped

a mortar and pestle

2 metal skewers

Serves 1

To make the chermoula, use a mortar and pestle to pound
the garlic with the salt to a smooth paste. Add the cumin,
chilli/chile, lemon juice and olive oil and stir in the
coriander/cilantro.

Put the fish chunks in a shallow dish and rub with the
chermoula. Cover and chill in the fridge for 1–2 hours.

Thread the monkfish and cherry tomatoes alternately onto
the skewers. Preheat your grill/broiler to high. Cook the kebabs
for about 3 minutes on each side, until the monkfish is nicely
browned. Dust with a little paprika and enjoy with a few
spoonfuls of cooked rice and a wedge of lemon for squeezing.

Serve these delicious veggie skewers with a couscous or quinoa and a good spoonful of the herby tapenade. Any extra tapenade will keep well in the fridge covered with a layer of oil, and is also very good eaten with grilled white fish or chicken.

chargrilled halloumi with mixed olive and herb tapenade

125 g/4½ oz. halloumi cheese

½ red bell pepper

½ courgette/zucchini

½ teaspoon coriander seeds

½ teaspoon cumin seeds

½ garlic clove, crushed

'a pinch of dried oregano

1 tablespoon olive oil

salt and freshly ground
black pepper

couscous or quinoa, to serve
(optional)

For the tapenade

4 tablespoons mixed pitted olives

½ small preserved lemon,
rind only

2 tablespoons chopped flat-leaf
parsley leaves

1 tablespoon chopped mint leaves

1 garlic clove

4 tablespoons fruity extra virgin
olive oil

2–3 wooden skewers

a pestle and mortar

a food processor

Serves 1

Cut the halloumi into chunks and place in a shallow dish. Cut the red bell pepper and courgette/zucchini into chunks the same size as the halloumi and add to the dish.

Toast the coriander and cumin seeds in a dry frying pan/skillet over medium heat for about 1 minute, or until aromatic. Crush lightly using a pestle and mortar and add to the halloumi and vegetables. Add the garlic, oregano and olive oil. Season with black pepper, mix well to combine and set aside to marinate for an hour or so. Meanwhile, soak the wooden skewers in water so that they don't burn when you cook them.

To make the tapenade, tip all the ingredients into a food processor and process until combined and roughly chopped. Taste and add black pepper and salt if necessary, but remember that the halloumi is quite salty already.

Preheat a ridged stovetop griddle/grill pan. Thread the marinated halloumi, courgettes/zucchini and peppers onto the wooden skewers, making sure that each one has an even amount of vegetables and cheese. Cook the skewers in the hot pan in batches until golden and the cheese has softened. Enjoy with couscous or quinoa and the tapenade on the side for spooning.

A reminder that taco fillings need not be complex, these are filled with simply cooked chicken. For an easier option, feel free to shred a ready-roasted chicken instead of cooking your own (and use the leftovers for plenty more meals; see page 40). This simple recipe is the perfect opportunity to serve up a variety of delicious deli salsas and sides.

shredded chicken tacos

200 g/7 oz. boneless, skinless chicken

chicken or vegetable stock, or water, as needed

2–3 soft tacos or small soft flour tortillas

50 g/¼ cup crumbled feta cheese or Mexican queso fresco

salt and freshly ground black pepper

To serve

deli-bought sides, such as fresh tomato salsa and guacamole

sprigs of coriander/cilantro

hot sauce (such as Tabasco)

a lime wedge

Serves 1

Put the chicken in a saucepan and add enough stock or water to cover. If using water or unseasoned stock, season with salt.

Bring to the boil over medium heat, then cover and simmer gently for 20–30 minutes until cooked through and tender. Remove the chicken from the pan and let cool slightly, then shred using your hands or two forks. Taste and adjust the seasoning.

To eat, put a generous helping of the shredded chicken in the centre of each taco and sprinkle over a handful of crumbled cheese. Top with spoonfuls of deli-bought sides and a sprig of coriander/cilantro, with hot sauce and halved limes for squeezing. All of this is best done with your hands!

This recipe makes 4 servings of the versatile burrito filling so that you can freeze the rest to enjoy another day as a filling for a baked sweet potato or with rice and guacamole.

chorizo, bean and pepper burrito

1 tablespoon vegetable oil

1 large onion, diced

1 red or yellow bell pepper, diced

2 garlic cloves, crushed

1 teaspoon dried oregano

½ teaspoon dried chilli/hot red pepper flakes

225 g/8 oz. chorizo, diced

400-g/14-oz. can chopped tomatoes

400-g/14-oz. can cannellini beans, drained

salt and freshly ground black pepper

1 large soft flour tortilla per serving

250 g/2½ cups grated Cheddar or Monterey Jack cheese

sour cream, to serve

Serves 1-4 (see recipe introduction)

Preheat the oven to 200°C (400°F) Gas 6.

Heat the oil in a large frying pan/skillet set over medium–high heat. Add the onion and bell pepper and cook for 5–8 minutes, stirring occasionally, until browned. Add the garlic, oregano, dried chilli/hot pepper flakes and chorizo and cook for 1–2 minutes. Add the tomatoes, beans, 4 tablespoons water and season with salt and pepper. Cook for about 15 minutes, stirring occasionally, until thickened. Taste and adjust the seasoning. (Let cool and freeze any you aren't using in individual portions at this stage.)

To prepare a burrito, spoon a quarter of the filling onto a tortilla and sprinkle with grated cheese. Fold in the sides of the tortilla to cover the filling, then roll up to enclose. Place the filled tortilla seam-side down in a shallow baking dish. Cover with foil and bake in the preheated oven for 10–15 minutes just to warm through and melt the cheese. Serve hot with sour cream on the side.

Serve these for brunch, lunch or dinner, with rice and refried beans if you need something more substantial. The quantities can easily be reduced to a single serving, or make a batch.

chicken and chorizo quesadilla

650 g/1 lb 7 oz. boneless, skinless chicken

chicken or vegetable stock, or water, as required

2 tablespoons vegetable oil

1 onion, finely chopped

2 garlic cloves, finely chopped

1 teaspoon ground cumin

1 teaspoon dried oregano

1 teaspoon salt

1 fresh green chilli/chile, finely chopped

70 g/2 oz. chorizo, finely chopped

400-g/14-oz. can chopped tomatoes

1 large soft flour tortilla per serving

grated Cheddar or Monterey Jack cheese, to serve

sour cream, to serve

deli-bought guacamole, to serve

Serves 1-4 (see recipe introduction)

Put the chicken in a pan and add enough stock or water to cover. Season with salt if using water. Bring to the boil over medium heat, then simmer, covered, for 30–40 minutes until cooked through. Remove the chicken and let cool, then shred it using your hands or two forks. Season with salt and pepper.

Heat 1 tablespoon of the oil in a saucepan over medium–high heat. Add the onion and cook for 5–8 minutes, stirring occasionally, until golden. Add the garlic, cumin, oregano, salt, chilli/chile and chorizo and cook for 1–2 minutes, stirring frequently. Stir in the tomatoes and cover. Simmer for 15 minutes, then uncover and cook for 10–20 minutes until reduced. (Let cool and freeze any you aren't using in individual portions at this stage.)

To assemble a quesadilla, spread a quarter of the chicken mixture on a tortilla. Sprinkle with cheese and fold the tortilla over. Heat the remaining oil in a non-stick frying pan/skillet set over medium heat. When hot, add the quesadilla, lower the heat and cook for 2–3 minutes until golden on one side and the cheese begins to melt. Turn over and cook on the other side for 2–3 minutes. Cut into wedges and eat immediately, with sour cream and guacamole on the side.

The smoky taste of chipotle is irresistible mixed with the warmth of the cinnamon and the salty tang of the cheese. For an authentic Mexican taste, replace the feta with queso fresco.

chipotle, black bean and feta quesadilla

3 tablespoons vegetable oil

1 onion, diced

3 garlic cloves, crushed

1 teaspoon dried oregano

1 teaspoon ground cumin

a pinch of ground cinnamon

2 chipotle chillies/chiles in adobo sauce, finely chopped

200 g/1 cup passata (Italian sieved tomatoes)

2 x 400-g/14-oz. cans black beans, drained

a pinch of salt

1 large soft flour tortilla per serving

feta cheese or queso fresco, crumbled, to serve

sour cream, to serve

a mixture of chopped tomato, red onion and coriander, to serve

Serves 1-4 (see recipe introduction left)

Preheat the oven to 120°C (250°F) Gas ½.

Heat 2 tablespoons of the oil in a saucepan set over medium–high heat. Add the onion and cook for 5–8 minutes, stirring occasionally, until golden. Add the garlic, oregano, cumin and cinnamon and cook for 1–2 minutes, stirring often. Add the chopped chillies/chiles and cook for 1 minute further, stirring often. Stir in the passata, beans, a pinch of salt and 60 ml/¼ cup water and cover. Simmer for 15 minutes, then taste and adjust the seasoning. (Let cool and freeze any you aren't using in individual portions at this stage.)

To assemble a quesadilla, spread a quarter of the bean mixture on a tortilla. Sprinkle with feta and fold the tortilla over. Heat the remaining oil in a non-stick frying pan/skillet set over medium heat. When hot, add the quesadilla, lower the heat and cook for 2–3 minutes until golden on one side and the cheese begins to melt. Turn over and cook on the other side for 2–3 minutes.

To serve, top the quesadilla with the tomato and onion mixture. Cut into wedges and eat immediately.

This satisfying recipe is the burger interpretation of a traditional chilli con carne. These deliciously spicy burgers are good served with oven-baked fries and cooling sour cream for dipping.

chilli con carne burger

For 2 burgers

1 tablespoon olive oil

1–2 long thin strips of courgette/zucchini (optional)

200 g/7 oz. lean minced/ground beef

2 tablespoons chopped cooked kidney beans

4 teaspoons tomato purée/paste

½ red onion, finely chopped

3 tablespoons fresh breadcrumbs

1 tablespoon beaten egg

1 fresh red chilli/chile, finely chopped

a pinch of ground cumin

salt and freshly ground black pepper

For 1 serving

2 thin slices Cheddar cheese

1 wholemeal/whole-wheat bread roll, sliced

a few tablespoons of sour cream

oven-baked chips/fries (optional)

Makes 2 burgers (one can be frozen for another time)

Preheat the grill/broiler to medium.

Heat the oil in a ridged stovetop griddle/grill pan. Add the courgette/zucchini slices (if using) and cook over high heat, turning occasionally, until browned on each side. Set aside to cool.

Put the beef in a bowl with the kidney beans, tomato purée/paste, onion, breadcrumbs, egg, chilli/chile, cumin and salt and pepper. Work together with your hands until evenly mixed. Divide the beef mixture in half and shape into 2 burger patties. Squeeze them together to keep the ingredients well packed inside, then press each burger down to make them nice and flat. One of the burgers can be wrapped in clingfilm/plastic wrap and frozen at this point.

Put the burger on a baking sheet and grill/broil for 5 minutes on each side until cooked through. When the burger is cooked, remove from the grill/broiler, top with cheese slices and wrap the slices of courgette/zucchini around the burger.

Eat the burger straightaway sandwiched in a bun with oven-baked chips/fries and some sour cream on the side.

This recipe includes a very quick cheat's chilli con carne, which is pretty perfect, but if you have leftover chilli con carne this sandwich will put it to good use. Any nutty-tasting alpine cheese works well here, or even a Dutch cheese, but nothing too strong, as it will be overpowered by the spicy meat.

chilli bacon swiss cheese sandwich

3 rashers/slices streaky/American bacon

2 thick slices white bread

butter, softened, for spreading

sliced or grated Emmental/Swiss cheese

For the chilli con carne

½ small onion, finely chopped

1 tablespoon vegetable oil

100 g/3½ oz. minced/ground beef

½ teaspoon dried oregano

1 teaspoon ground cumin

¼ teaspoon chilli/hot red pepper flakes, or more to taste

¼ teaspoon ground cayenne pepper, or more to taste

100 g/3½ oz. passata (Italian sieved tomatoes)

200-g/7-oz. can black beans, drained

salt and freshly ground black pepper

Serves 1

For the chilli con carne, combine the onion and oil in a frying pan/skillet over medium heat and cook until soft and golden. Add the beef, herbs and spices and salt and pepper and cook, stirring occasionally, until browned. Add the passata/strained tomatoes and beans and simmer gently for at least 15 minutes. The mixture should be thick but not too thick; add a splash of water if necessary. Taste and adjust the seasoning.

Meanwhile, fry the bacon until crispy. Pat dry on paper towels and set aside. Spread some softened butter on one side of the bread slices.

This is easiest if assembled in a large heavy-based non-stick frying pan/skillet. Place a slice of bread in the pan/skillet, butter-side down. Top it with cheese, bacon and chilli con carne. It is best to drop the chilli con carne in spoonfuls and then spread the blobs out to the edges, gently, without disturbing the cheese beneath too much. Enclose with the remaining bread slice, butter-side up.

Turn the heat to medium and cook the first side for 3–5 minutes until deep golden, pressing down gently with a spatula. Carefully turn with a large spatula and cook on the other side, for 2–3 minutes more or until deep golden brown all over.

Remove from the pan, transfer to a plate and cut in half. Let cool for a few minutes before serving.

This is a French recipe which traditionally calls for Gruyère cheese only, but the blue cheese used here makes it even better and it's a good way to use up small leftover amounts. You can experiment with different kinds of ham; cured ham works especially well. Or, omit the ham altogether for an indulgent vegetarian supper. Serve with lots of crusty bread or boiled new potatoes and a crisp green salad on the side.

chicory gratin with ham and blue cheese

2 heads chicory/Belgian endive (about 90 g/3 oz. each), rinsed and dried

½ tablespoon olive oil

4 slices smoked ham

1 tablespoon freshly grated Gruyère or Parmesan cheese

salt

For the béchamel sauce

1 tablespoon butter

2 teaspoons plain/all-purpose flour

200 ml/¾ cup hot milk

a pinch of sea salt

¼ teaspoon paprika

25 g/1 oz. grated Gruyère cheese

15 g/1 tablespoon crumbled firm blue cheese

a small baking dish, well buttered

Serves 1

Preheat the oven to 200°C (400°F) Gas 6.

Halve the chicory/Belgian endive heads lengthways. Drizzle with the oil and rub with your hands to coat evenly. Arrange in a single layer on a baking sheet. Sprinkle lightly with salt and drizzle over about 2 tablespoons water. Roast in the preheated oven for about 15 minutes until just tender when pierced with a knife. Remove from the oven and let cool. Leave the oven on.

Meanwhile, prepare the béchamel sauce. Melt the butter in a heavy-based saucepan. Stir in the flour and cook, stirring constantly, for 1 minute. Pour in the hot milk gradually, whisking constantly and continue whisking gently for 3–5 minutes, until the sauce begins to thicken. Season with salt and paprika and add both the cheeses. Stir well to combine.

As soon as the chicory heads are cool enough to handle, carefully wrap each one with a slice of ham and arrange them side by side, seam-side down, in the prepared baking dish. Pour over the béchamel, spreading evenly to coat. Sprinkle with the grated cheese and bake in the still-hot oven for about 20–25 minutes, until browned and bubbling. Eat immediately with a leafy green salad and crusty bread.

These hearty vegetable burgers don't require a bun because they are packed full of filling starchy vegetables. It's a great way to use up any odds and ends from the fridge.

cheesy root vegetable burgers with mustard mayo

For the burgers

⅓ butternut squash, peeled and chopped

1 sweet potato, peeled and chopped

1 small potato, peeled and chopped

1 carrot, peeled and chopped

½ red onion, chopped

1 garlic clove, chopped

a large pinch of dried thyme

40 g/⅓ cup grated mature/sharp Cheddar cheese

salt and freshly ground black pepper

To serve

50 ml/¼ cup mayonnaise

1 teaspoon wholegrain or Dijon mustard

steamed green vegetables

Serves 1

Bring a large saucepan of water to the boil. Put the squash, sweet potato, potato, carrot, onion and garlic in the water and simmer for about 10 minutes, until soft. Drain well and mash with a potato masher. Add the thyme and salt and pepper and work together with your hands until evenly mixed.

Divide the mixture in half and shape into 2 burger patties. Press each burger down to make them nice and flat and roll each one in the grated cheese, so that it sticks all around the outside of each burger.

Preheat the grill/broiler to medium–hot.

Put the burgers on a greased baking sheet and grill/broil for 6–8 minutes on each side, until the cheese is brown and bubbling. Remove from the oven, check that the burgers are hot in the middle and let cool slightly before eating.

Meanwhile, mix the mayonnaise with the mustard in a small dish. Enjoy the burgers with the mustard mayo on the side and a side of steamed green vegetables, such as broccoli or green beans.

chapter 4

home-cooked comforts

warming one-bowl winners

This rich-tasting Bolognese sauce is much quicker to prepare than a traditional one, and the bacon helps to achieve the same delicious taste and unctuous texture. You can easily scale down the quantities, but it's very handy to keep in the freezer for stand-by suppers.

bolognese sauce

2 tablespoons olive oil or vegetable oil

1 large onion, finely chopped

3 celery stalks, finely chopped

2 large carrots, peeled and finely chopped

3 rashers/slices smoked bacon, finely chopped

1 teaspoon dried thyme

4 garlic cloves, finely chopped

500 g/1 lb 2 oz. minced/ ground beef

2 teaspoons sea salt

125 ml/½ cup red or white wine

2 litres/8 cups passata (Italian sieved tomatoes)

1 bay leaf

1 tablespoon sugar

salt and freshly ground black pepper

To serve

cooked spaghetti

a handful of small basil leaves

finely grated Parmesan cheese (optional)

Makes 6 servings (can be frozen for another time)

Heat the oil in a large heavy-based saucepan or casserole dish. Add the onion, celery, carrots and bacon and fry over a medium heat for about 10 minutes, stirring occasionally, until softened and well coloured, taking care not to burn.

Stir in the thyme and garlic, increase the heat and add the beef. Cook for 3–5 minutes, stirring occasionally, until browned. Add the salt and wine and bring to the boil. Boil for 1 minute to cook off the alcohol.

Add the passata, bay leaf and sugar and stir well. Reduce the heat, cover with a lid and simmer the Bolognese sauce for 1–1½ hours until it is rich and thickened, stirring occasionally. Taste and adjust the seasoning and remove the bay leaf. (Let cool and freeze any you aren't using in individual portions at this stage.)

Spoon into a warmed serving bowl of hot spaghetti and sprinkle with basil leaves and Parmesan.

This is a traditional Moroccan recipe. This recipe makes 4 servings of sauce and meatballs which can be frozen separately and enjoyed another time. You can add sliced cooked pork or vegetarian sausages to the reheated sauce and serve it with mashed potatoes and green beans. The meatballs can be defrosted and cooked using the same method as here in any tomato-based sauce and are good served on a mound of hot spaghetti with plenty of freshly grated Parmesan.

spicy lamb meatball tagine

For the meatballs

½ onion, coarsely chopped

a few sprigs of flat-leaf parsley

a few sprigs of coriander/cilantro

500 g/1 lb 2 oz. minced/ground lamb

1½ teaspoons salt

½ teaspoon ground white pepper

1 teaspoon ground cumin

1 teaspoon paprika

1 tablespoon fresh breadcrumbs

1 egg per serving (optional)

For the spicy tomato sauce

1½ white onions

a small handful of flat-leaf parsley

2 garlic cloves

400-g/14-oz can chopped tomatoes

300 ml/1¼ cups stock (chicken, lamb or vegetable) or water

1½ teaspoons ground cumin

1 teaspoon ground white pepper

¼ teaspoon ground cinnamon

¼–½ teaspoon cayenne pepper, to taste

a pinch of sugar

a food processor

Makes 4 servings (see recipe introduction)

To make the meatballs, put the onion in a food processor with the parsley and coriander/cilantro. Process until finely chopped. Add the lamb and process, using the pulse button, to obtain a smooth paste. Transfer to a bowl. Add the salt, pepper, cumin, paprika and breadcrumbs. Mix well with your hands to combine. Form into walnut-size balls and transfer to a baking sheet. (You will want 4–6 meatballs for one serving. Freeze any meatballs you aren't using now at this stage.)

To make the sauce, put the onions, parsley and garlic in a food processor and process until finely chopped. Transfer to a shallow frying pan/skillet large enough to hold the meatballs in a single layer. Add the tomatoes, stock, cumin, pepper, cinnamon, cayenne and sugar. Stir and bring to the boil, then lower the heat and simmer, covered, for 15 minutes. (You will need a quarter of the sauce for 1 serving. Let cool and freeze any you aren't using in individual portions at this stage.)

Nestle the meatballs in the sauce in a single layer. Cover and simmer for 20–30 minutes, until cooked through.

To serve, put some meatballs and sauce in a shallow soup plate or large bowl, arranging the meatballs in a ring around the perimeter. Poach or lightly fry an egg, if using, (keep the yolks runny) and place one cooked egg in the middle of the bowl. Eat immediately with crusty bread to mop up the sauce.

This is an Italian take on sausage and mash with a bit of British redcurrant jelly thrown in to make the onion gravy deliciously sticky. If you've tried polenta before and weren't blown away, try it again now: the secret, as with most of the good things in life, is lots of butter, cheese and seasoning.

herby sausages with polenta and rosemary, red onion and redcurrant gravy

2–3 good-quality herby sausages

For the gravy

½ tablespoon olive oil

½ red onion, thinly sliced

½ rosemary sprig, broken up

1 teaspoon plain/all-purpose flour

½ tablespoon redcurrant jelly

75 ml/⅓ cup red wine

75 ml/⅓ cup beef stock

1 teaspoon butter

For the polenta

40 g/1¼ cup quick-cook polenta

1 tablespoon butter

20 g/⅓ cup freshly grated Parmesan cheese

salt and freshly ground black pepper

Serves 1

Put 200 ml/¾ cup water in a medium pan over high heat, cover and heat until it simmers. Pour the polenta into the pan of simmering water and beat out any lumps. Reduce the heat to low and bubble away for 30 minutes, or according to the manufacturer's instructions.

To make the gravy, heat the olive oil in a frying pan/skillet and start cooking the onion and rosemary over medium heat, stirring. When the onion begins to soften, reduce the heat, cover and leave to soften slowly in its own juices. After 5–10 minutes, stir in the flour and cook for about 1 minute until it is no longer pale. Add the jelly, wine and stock and bring to the boil. Leave to bubble away gently for 10 minutes while you cook the sausages.

Preheat the grill/broiler. Put the sausages on a baking sheet lined with foil and grill/broil for 15 minutes, turning halfway through.

When everything is ready, beat the butter and Parmesan into the polenta and season with salt and pepper. Beat the butter into the gravy and season to taste. Transfer the polenta to a serving bowl, top with the sausages, pour over the hot gravy and enjoy.

Chow mein is a classic noodle stir-fry that should be part of every keen cook's repertoire. Treat this recipe as a basic guide to which you can add your own touches. Try varying the vegetables and replacing the beef with chicken or even tofu.

beef chow mein

150 g/5 oz. sirloin beef or fillet, trimmed of fat and very thinly sliced

150 g/5 oz. fresh medium egg noodles

¾ tablespoon groundnut/peanut oil

2 spring onions/scallions, finely chopped, white and green parts kept separately

85 g/3 oz. choy sum (or pak choi), chopped into 2-cm/¾-inch pieces, stalks and leaves kept separately

½ red chilli/chile, thinly sliced, to garnish (optional)

For the marinade

¾ tablespoon dark soy sauce

¼ tablespoon Chinese rice wine

¼ teaspoon sugar

1 small garlic clove, crushed

½ teaspoon finely grated fresh ginger

1 teaspoon cornflour/cornstarch

For the sauce

1 tablespoon oyster sauce

100 ml/scant ½ cup chicken stock

½ tablespoon light soy sauce

½ tablespoon dark soy sauce

1 teaspoon cornflour/cornstarch

Serves 1

Put the beef in a bowl, add all the marinade ingredients, mix well and set aside.

Bring a saucepan of water to the boil. Add the noodles and blanch for 2–3 minutes. Drain and rinse under cold running water, then set aside.

Combine all the sauce ingredients in a bowl and set aside.

Heat a little of the oil in a wok or large frying pan/skillet until hot. Add the marinated beef and stir-fry over high heat for 2–3 minutes, or until well seared all over. Remove the beef from the wok and set aside.

Heat the remaining oil in the wok, then add the white parts of the spring onions/scallions and stir-fry for just 30 seconds. Add the stalks of the choy sum and stir-fry for 2 minutes. Pour in the sauce and bring to the boil. Leave to bubble for 1 minute, then return the beef to the wok and stir through.

Stir the drained noodles into the wok and cook for 1–2 minutes, or until the noodles are tender. Transfer the chow mein to a deep serving bowl, garnish with the reserved green bits of the spring onions/scallions and the sliced chilli/chile, if using, and eat immediately.

The authentic flavour of a curry comes from using fresh spices and the heady, slightly sour taste of curry leaves. Chicken thigh fillets work better here than breast meat as they are harder to overcook. Make this in a larger quantity and freeze to enjoy another time.

chicken and lentil curry with cucumber yogurt

25 g/2 tablespoons butter

2 large onions, thinly sliced

2 garlic cloves, crushed

1½ tablespoons garam masala
(or ¼ teaspoon ground nutmeg,
½ teaspoon ground cinnamon,
½ teaspoon ground pepper,
1 teaspoon ground cumin and
10 cardamom pods, crushed)

500 g/1 lb 2 oz. chicken thigh
fillets or breast fillets, cut into
chunks

300 g/10½ oz. tomato passata
(Italian sieved tomatoes)

8 curry or 4 bay leaves

100 g/⅔ cup red lentils

400 ml/1¾ cups chicken stock

salt and freshly ground
black pepper

coriander/cilantro leaves, to
serve (optional)

mango chutney and warm
chapatis, to serve (optional)

For the cucumber yogurt

140 ml/⅔ cup plain yogurt

¼ cucumber, cut into ribbons
or chopped

**Makes 4 servings (the rest can
be frozen for another time)**

Melt the butter in a deep frying pan/skillet, add the onions and fry, stirring, over medium heat. Once they are sizzling, cover with a lid, reduce the heat and cook for 10–15 minutes, stirring occasionally.

When the onions have softened, add the garlic and garam masala and cook for a further 3–4 minutes, until the spices start to release their aroma and the onions are beginning to turn golden. If using chicken thighs, add them now and cook for 5–6 minutes. Add the passata, curry leaves, lentils and stock. If you are using chicken breast, add it now. Cover with a lid and simmer for 15 minutes until the lentils are tender.

To make the cucumber yogurt, put the yogurt in a small dish, add a good pinch of salt and stir in the cucumber.

When the curry is cooked, season generously with salt and black pepper. Lentils tend to absorb a lot of seasoning, so don't be stingy. (Let cool and freeze any you aren't using now in individual portions at this stage.)

Transfer to a serving bowl, scatter with coriander/cilantro, if using, and enjoy with a dollop of the cucumber yogurt to stir in. Serve with mango chutney and warm chapatis, rolled up, if liked.

Spicy and satisfying, this street-food dish packs in all the flavours of
Thailand. The shrimp paste adds a distinctive depth to the dish, so don't
let its pungent aroma put you off. And don't forget the squeeze of fresh
lime juice at the end for that essential tangy finish.

chicken pad thai

75 g/3 oz. dried flat Thai rice
noodles

1 large garlic clove, crushed

½ large red chilli/chile, deseeded
and finely chopped, plus ¼ finely
chopped, to serve

½ teaspoon shrimp paste
(optional)

½ tablespoon vegetable oil, plus
extra if needed

1 skinless chicken breast, cut
into 2-cm/¾-inch pieces

1 tablespoon fish sauce

1 egg, lightly beaten

50 g/2 oz. beansprouts

20 g/¾ oz. Chinese chives, cut
into 4-cm/1¾-inch lengths

½ tablespoon tamarind paste

½ tablespoon palm sugar or soft
light brown sugar

1½ tablespoons chopped roasted
peanuts

1 spring onion/scallion, green
and light green parts only, thinly
sliced on the diagonal

a squeeze of fresh lime juice

1 tablespoon roughly chopped
coriander/cilantro leaves

lime wedges, to serve

a food processor or mortar and
pestle

Serves 1

Put the noodles in a large heatproof bowl and cover with
boiling water. Soak for 20 minutes, or until softened but not
cooked through. Drain well.

Meanwhile, put the garlic, chilli/chile and shrimp paste, if
using, in a pestle and mortar and grind until you have a rough
paste. Alternatively, blitz in a food processor with a little water.

Heat the oil in a wok or large frying pan/skillet until very hot.
Add the paste and fry over high heat for 1 minute, or until
fragrant. Season the chicken with ¼ tablespoon of the fish
sauce and add to the wok. Stir-fry for 4 minutes, or until just
cooked through. Remove the cooked chicken from the wok
and set aside.

Heat another ¼ tablespoon oil in the wok, if necessary. When
hot, pour in the beaten egg. Leave the bottom to set, then
break up with a spoon to get softly set scrambled egg. Return
the chicken to the wok with the drained noodles, beansprouts
and Chinese chives. Stir well.

Meanwhile, combine the remaining fish sauce with the
tamarind paste and palm sugar, then add to the wok with half
the peanuts. Stir-fry for 2–4 minutes, or until the noodles are
tender. You may need to sprinkle in a little water if the noodles
look too dry. Stir in the spring onion/scallion and lime juice.
Taste and add more fish sauce if you think it needs it.

Transfer the pad Thai to a serving plate, garnish with the
chopped coriander/cilantro, chilli/chile and remaining peanuts
and eat immediately with lime wedges for squeezing.

This sophisticated take on the classic combination of ham, cheese and pasta uses smoked mozzarella, which was made to be melted. The result is a velvety texture interspersed with salty chunks of ham hock.

ham and smoked mozzarella rigatoni

250 g/9 oz. rigatoni

100 g/3½ oz. cooked ham hock, shredded

125 g/4½ oz. smoked mozzarella cheese, finely sliced

4 quantities Béchamel Sauce (page 82), replacing the Gruyère and blue cheese with 50 g/scant ½ cup grated Cheddar cheese

25 g/½ cup fresh breadcrumbs

salt and freshly ground black pepper

Makes 3–4 servings (the rest can be frozen for another time)

Bring a pan of salted water to the boil and cook the pasta according to the instructions on the packet, until al dente.

Combine the ham hock and half the mozzarella and mix well. Taste and adjust the seasoning. Set aside.

Preheat the grill/broiler to medium.

Prepare the béchamel sauce (see page 82), remove from the heat and add the cheese, mixing well with a spoon to incorporate.

Put the cooked pasta in a large mixing bowl. Pour over the hot béchamel sauce and the ham mixture and mix well. Taste and adjust the seasoning.

Transfer the mixture to 3–4 baking dishes (use individual ones or small foil containers to make it easier to freeze in single servings) and spread it out evenly. Top with the remaining mozzarella and a good grinding of black pepper and sprinkle the breadcrumbs evenly over the top. Grill/broil for 5–10 minutes until the top is crunchy and golden brown. Eat immediately.

The best part of this is the way the crunchy sweetness of the fresh corn kernels is complemented by the smoky toasted cumin. You can use frozen or canned sweetcorn in this recipe, but it will not taste as good!

spicy corn mac 'n' cheese

250 g/9 oz. macaroni

2 fresh sweetcorn cobs

¾ teaspoon cumin seeds

4 quantities Béchamel Sauce (page 82), replacing the Gruyère and blue cheese with 100 g/scant 1 cup mixed grated Cheddar and Monterey Jack cheese

½ red chilli/chile, deseeded and finely diced

½ green chilli/chile, deseeded and finely diced

a few sprigs of coriander/cilantro, finely chopped

25 g/½ cup fresh breadcrumbs

salt and freshly ground black pepper

a mortar and pestle

Makes 3–4 servings (the rest can be frozen for another time)

Bring a pan of salted water to the boil and cook the macaroni according to the instructions on the packet, until al dente.

Bring another large pan of water to the boil. Add the corn cobs and cook for 3 minutes. Drain and let cool slightly, then scrape off the kernels with a sharp knife and set aside.

Heat a small frying pan/skillet until hot but not smoking. Add the cumin seeds and cook until aromatic and beginning to brown. Leave to cool, then grind to a powder with a mortar and pestle and set aside. Preheat the grill/broiler to medium.

Prepare the béchamel sauce (see page 82), remove from the heat and add the cheeses, chillies/chiles and cumin, mixing with a spoon to incorporate. Taste and adjust the seasoning.

Put the cooked macaroni in a large mixing bowl. Add the corn and coriander/cilantro, pour over the hot béchamel and mix well. Taste and adjust the seasoning.

Transfer the mixture to 3–4 baking dishes (use individual ones or small foil containers to make it easier to freeze in single servings) and spread evenly. Top with black pepper and sprinkle the breadcrumbs evenly over the top. Grill/broil for 5–10 minutes until the top is crunchy and golden brown. Eat immediately.

A classic of French home cooking, this gratin includes a topping of tangy goat cheese. If you grow your own herbs, add whatever is on offer: savory, majoram, oregano or any other soft-leaved herb, the more the merrier. This is perfect simply served with a mixed salad of lettuce and ripe tomatoes and some slices of fresh crusty bread.

courgette gratin with fresh herbs and goat cheese

65 ml/¼ cup double/heavy cream

leaves from a few sprigs of flat-leaf parsley, finely chopped

a small sprig of chives, snipped

a pinch of freshly grated nutmeg

20 g/1 oz. Gruyère cheese, grated

350 g/12 oz. courgettes/zucchini, very thinly sliced

40 g/1½ oz. soft goat cheese

salt and freshly ground black pepper

a small round, deep-sided baking dish, well buttered

Serves 1

Preheat the oven to 190°C (375°F) Gas 5.

Put the cream, parsley, chives, nutmeg, salt and pepper in a small bowl and whisk together. Add half the Gruyère cheese.

Arrange half the courgette/zucchini slices in the prepared baking dish, sprinkle with the remaining Gruyère and season with a little salt. Top with the remaining courgette/zucchini slices, season again and pour over the cream mixture. Crumble the goat cheese over the top.

Bake in the preheated oven for 20–25 minutes, or until browned and bubbling. Enjoy immediately with a mixed salad and slices of fresh crusty bread.

A bit like a mac 'n' cheese fish pie, this hearty and nutritious recipe makes a perfect weeknight meal for anyone with a healthy appetite. Serve with plenty of fresh green vegetables such as peas or steamed broccoli florets.

salmon, basil and parmesan pasta bake

170 g/6 oz. any tube pasta shape

170 g/6 oz. boneless, skinless salmon fillets

200 ml/¾ cup double/heavy cream

leaves from a small bunch of basil, chopped, reserving a few whole leaves to serve

75 g/⅔ cup grated medium Cheddar cheese

30 g/¼ cup grated Parmesan

15 g/⅓ cup fresh breadcrumbs

salt and freshly ground black pepper

Makes 2 servings (freeze or chill one to eat later)

Bring a pan of salted water to the boil and cook the pasta according to the instructions on the packet, until al dente.

Preheat the oven to 200°C (400°F) Gas 6.

Put the salmon fillet on a baking sheet and bake until cooked through and the flesh flakes easily. Remove and let cool slightly.

Preheat the grill/broiler to medium–hot. Put the cream and basil in a saucepan and bring just to the boil, stirring occasionally. Remove from the heat, add the cheeses and stir well to melt.

Flake the salmon and put it in a large bowl. Add the cooked pasta, pour over the hot cream sauce and mix well. Taste and season with salt and pepper. Transfer the mixture to 2 small baking dishes and spread evenly. Top each one with a good grinding of black pepper and sprinkle the breadcrumbs evenly over the top. (Wrap one in foil and chill or freeze ready to cook another time.)

Grill/broil the other one for 5–10 minutes, until the top is crunchy and golden brown. Scatter over the remaining basil leaves and eat immediately.

Inspired by a traditional Greek dish, this is simple yet elegant, and as good for a quick midweek supper as it is for an indulgent treat.

prawn and feta pasta bake

170 g/6 oz. any tube or ridged pasta shape

1 tablespoon vegetable oil

½ large onion, finely diced

100 g/3½ oz. raw prawns/shrimp

½ teaspoon dried thyme

½ teaspoon dried oregano

½ teaspoon salt

1 garlic clove, crushed

200 g/7 oz. canned chopped tomatoes

double quantity Béchamel Sauce (page 82), replacing the cheese with 30 g/¼ cup grated Graviera or Gruyère and 75 g/⅔ cup grated Cheddar

30 g/¼ cup crumbled feta

salt and freshly ground black pepper

Makes 2 servings (cooked prawns/shrimp are not suitable for freezing, see page 4, so cover and chill one serving to heat and serve the next day)

Bring a pan of salted water to the boil and cook the pasta according to the instructions on the packet until al dente.

Heat the oil in a large sauté pan with a lid. Add the onion and cook over medium heat for 5 minutes, until just golden. Stir in the prawns/shrimp, thyme, oregano and salt and cook until the prawns/shrimp just turn pink. Add the garlic and cook gently for 1 minute, taking care not to let it burn. Add the tomatoes and a grinding of black pepper and simmer very gently for about 15–30 minutes, until the mixture has reduced to a jam-like consistency.

Preheat the grill/broiler to medium.

Prepare the béchamel sauce (see page 82), remove from the heat and add the cheeses, mixing well with a spoon to incorporate. Taste and season with salt and pepper.

Put the cooked pasta in a mixing bowl. Pour over the hot béchamel sauce and mix well. Taste the prawn/shrimp mixture and adjust the seasoning as necessary. Add to the pasta and mix well. Transfer the mixture to two individual baking dishes and spread evenly. Sprinkle over the feta and grill/broil for 5–10 minutes until the top is browned. Eat immediately. To reheat the other serving, bake in a moderate oven for about 25 minutes and finish under the grill as directed above, for a crispy top.

105

This is an ideal weeknight meal when supplies run low since it can be made almost entirely from storecupboard and freezer ingredients. For a bit of additional greenery, you could throw in a large handful of defrosted frozen peas just before serving, or top with a few finely sliced spring onions/scallions for added crunch.

seafood curry

½ tablespoon vegetable oil

½ onion, finely chopped

1 garlic clove, crushed

a small piece of fresh ginger, grated

¼ fresh red chilli/chile, deseeded and finely chopped

¼ teaspoon ground turmeric

½ teaspoon ground cumin

½ teaspoon ground coriander

¼ teaspoon hot paprika

100 ml/⅓ cup canned coconut milk

200 g/7 oz. peeled prawns/shrimp, fresh or frozen

a handful of coriander/cilantro leaves, finely chopped

salt and freshly ground black pepper

cooked basmati rice, to serve

a few sprigs of coriander/cilantro, to serve

Serves 1

Heat the oil in a large heavy-based frying pan/skillet or deep sauté dish. Add the onion and cook over medium heat for 3–5 minutes until just soft. Stir in the garlic, ginger, chilli/chile, turmeric, cumin, coriander and paprika and cook for 1 minute, stirring continuously.

Add the coconut milk and bring to the boil. Add the prawns/shrimp, reduce the heat to simmer and cook gently for 10 minutes, or until they are cooked through.

Remove the prawns/shrimp from the sauce and whisk the sauce well to thicken it. Taste and season with salt and pepper if necessary. Stir in the chopped coriander/cilantro and garnish with sprigs of coriander/cilantro to serve, with cooked basmati rice, if liked.

special suppers

indulgent dishes for when you have more time

This sticky glaze is quick and easy to put together with things you are likely to already have in your kitchen cupboard and livens up a simple pork escalope no end. It can also be brushed onto chicken breasts and other meats ahead of grilling. It's best to add the peas and yogurt to the potatoes just before you plan to eat them.

curry glazed pork escalope with spiced potatoes and peas

¼ tablespoon Madras curry paste

½ tablespoon mango chutney

½ teaspoon ground turmeric

½ tablespoon sunflower oil

1 lean loin pork escalope (weighing about 150 g/5 oz.), trimmed of fat

3–5 sweet cherry tomatoes, attached to the vine

salt and freshly ground black pepper

For the spiced potatoes and peas

150 g/5 oz. potatoes, peeled and diced

½ tablespoon sunflower oil

2 teaspoons butter

½ small onion, finely chopped

¼ garlic clove, crushed

¼ teaspoon cumin seeds

40 g/⅓ cup frozen petits pois

½ tablespoon Greek yogurt

salt

Serves 1

First make the spiced potatoes and peas. Cook the potatoes for 10 minutes in a pan of boiling salted water. Drain in a colander. Heat the oil and butter in a frying pan/skillet and add the onion, garlic and cumin seeds. Cook over low heat until the onions have softened. Add the potatoes and 100 ml/⅓ cup water, and continue to cook until the potatoes are tender, about 10 minutes.

Meanwhile, preheat the grill/broiler to high and cover the rack in foil. Put the curry paste, mango chutney, turmeric and oil in a bowl and mix well. Season with salt and pepper. Put the escalope on the grill/broiler rack, season well and brush with half the curry mixture. Arrange the cherry tomatoes on the rack alongside the pork and drizzle with the remaining oil.

Cook the escalope and tomatoes under the preheated grill/broiler for 5–6 minutes, or until the pork is slightly charred. Brush the other side with the remaining curry mixture and cook for a further 5–6 minutes.

Add the peas and yogurt to the potatoes just before you are about to serve. Bring to the boil and let bubble for 1 minute.

To serve, spoon the spiced potatoes and peas onto a warmed serving plate and put the pork escalope on top along the tomatoes. Enjoy with a nice smooth glass of red wine.

Perfect as an indulgence for one, steak is an expensive ingredient, so here's what you need to do to get the best results. See opposite for delicious butters to serve with a simple steak and salad.

cooking steak: the basics

* Always start with your steak at room temperature. If it's straight from the fridge, the short cooking time in some recipes could leave the centre of the meat cold.

* Trim off any visible fat. Most steaks are cooked too quickly to cook the fat through and you will probably prefer to cut it off before you eat it anyway.

* Pat the meat dry with paper towels before cooking so that it will brown, particularly if it has been vacuum-packed or stored in a plastic bag. Even if you have marinated the steak beforehand, dry it before you cook it or it will simmer rather than sizzle.

* If you are frying steak, make sure the frying pan/skillet is hot before you begin. A ridged stove-top griddle/grill pan should be very hot. However, if you are frying in oil and butter or cooking a steak coated in peppercorns or a spicy rub, you'll need to reduce the heat slightly as these can catch and burn if the temperature is too high. When using a stove-top griddle/grill pan or barbecue, oil the steak rather than the pan or rack.

* Always rest your steak, lightly covered, on a warm plate for at least 3 minutes after cooking. This is very important, as it results in a much more tender, juicier steak.

how long should you cook a steak for?

This depends how thick the steak is and how well cooked you like it. Steaks are generally cooked medium-rare or rare, which is how most people prefer them, although a few hardened carnivores like their steaks 'blue' – simply shown the pan and barely cooked at all. However, that doesn't suit most steak dishes. If you prefer your steak medium to well done, simply add a minute or two to the cooking times in the recipe.

Delicious butters can be kept in the fridge or freezer to provide an instant topping for steak (or other grilled meats and fish). Serve cool rather than chilled, so they melt on contact with hot food. All recipes make 6 portions.

flavoured butters

chilli, lime and coriander butter

110 g/½ cup butter, softened

1 tablespoon freshly squeezed lime juice

2 garlic cloves, crushed

2 small red chillies/chiles, deseeded and very finely chopped

1 teaspoon finely grated lime zest

¼ teaspoon sweet pimentón (Spanish oak-smoked paprika)

1½ tablespoons finely chopped coriander/cilantro leaves

flaky sea salt

Beat the butter with a wooden spoon or an electric hand-held mixer until light and smooth, then gradually work in the lime juice. Add the garlic, chillies/chiles, lime zest, pimentón, coriander/cilantro and a good pinch of salt flakes, rubbed between your fingers.

Spoon the butter onto a piece of kitchen foil and shape it into a rectangle. Roll up the foil into a sausage shape and twist the ends like a Christmas cracker, then chill until firm. Remove from the fridge 20–30 minutes before serving 1 or 2 slices on a steak or hot food.

blue cheese, cracked pepper and chive butter

100 g/3½ oz. creamy blue cheese, such as Gorgonzola, Fourme d'Ambert or Cashel Blue

100 g/scant ½ cup butter, softened

1 teaspoon black peppercorns, crushed

1 tablespoon finely snipped chives

Cut the cheese and butter into chunks, removing any rind from the cheese, and put in a bowl. Beat together with a wooden spoon or an electric hand-held mixer, then add the crushed peppercorns and chives and mix thoroughly.

Spoon the butter onto a piece of kitchen foil and shape it into a rectangle. Roll up into a sausage shape and twist the ends like a Christmas cracker, then chill until firm. Remove from the fridge 20–30 minutes before serving 1 or 2 slices on hot food.

lemon, garlic and parsley butter

1 garlic clove, chopped

¼ teaspoon fine sea salt

125 g/generous ½ cup butter, softened

1 tablespoon freshly squeezed lemon juice

½ teaspoon finely grated lemon zest

3 tablespoons finely chopped parsley

freshly ground black pepper

Crush the garlic and salt to a smooth paste in a pestle and mortar. Beat the butter until light and smooth, then gradually work in the lemon juice. Add the garlic , lemon zest and parsley and beat thoroughly. Season with a little black pepper.

Spoon the butter onto a piece of kitchen foil and shape it into a rectangle. Roll up the foil into a sausage shape and twist the ends like a Christmas cracker, then chill until firm. Remove from the fridge 20–30 minutes before serving 1 or 2 slices on hot food.

This is a great way of using up any unused steak from another recipe. You can, of course, use a store-bought teriyaki marinade to save time.

teriyaki steak with noodles

85 g/3 oz. rump or sirloin steak, sliced about 1 cm/½ inch thick

1 tablespoon sunflower or rapeseed/canola oil

½ red bell pepper, quartered, cored and cut into strips

25 g/1 oz. shiitake mushrooms, rinsed and halved

25 g/1 oz. sugar snap peas

2–3 spring onions/scallions, trimmed and cut into 4-cm/1¾-inch lengths

100 g/3½ oz. dried egg noodles

sansho pepper or coarsely ground black pepper

For the marinade

1 tablespoon Japanese soy sauce

1 tablespoon sake

½ tablespoon mirin (Japanese rice wine)

½ teaspoon unrefined caster/granulated sugar

½ small garlic clove, crushed

Serves 1

To make the marinade, mix the ingredients in a shallow bowl. Trim the steak of any excess fat or sinews and cut into strips about 1.5 cm/⅝ inch wide. Toss the strips of steak in the marinade, then cover and set aside for 1 hour.

When ready to cook, remove the meat from the marinade and pat dry with paper towels. Heat a wok over high heat for a couple of minutes, add half the sunflower oil and swirl around the pan. Add the meat and stir-fry briefly on both sides. Add a couple of tablespoons of the marinade and stir-fry for a few seconds more, then transfer to a warm plate.

Rinse the wok and dry with paper towels, then add the remaining oil and bell pepper strips and stir-fry over high heat for 1 minute. Add the rest of the vegetables and stir-fry for another 3–4 minutes. Pour in the remaining marinade and let bubble up until the liquid has reduced by half. Add 50 ml/3 tablespoons water to prevent the sauce tasting too salty.

Put the steak back in the pan together with any juices that have accumulated under the meat, stir-fry for a few seconds, then turn off the heat.

Meanwhile, bring a pan of salted water to the boil and cook the noodles according the instructions on the packet, then drain. Tip into a deep serving bowl and spoon over the meat and vegetables. Sprinkle with sansho pepper and eat immediately.

This is a cheat's version of a Spanish peasant stew called a *fabada*, which makes a welcoming supper on a cold winter's evening. If you can't get hold of chorizo, any spicy sausage will do. It is especially good with a nice big glass of Spanish Rioja.

spanish sausage and butter bean tagine

1 tablespoon olive oil

1 onion, finely chopped

2 garlic cloves, crushed

75 g/2½ oz. chorizo sausage, skin removed and cut into 1-cm/¼-inch slices

100 ml/⅓ cup red wine

400-g/14-oz. can chopped tomatoes

1 red onion, cut into thin petals

400-g/14-oz. can butter beans, drained

1 teaspoon dried mixed herbs

a few rosemary or thyme sprigs

2 tablespoons finely grated Parmesan cheese

salt and freshly ground black pepper

warm crusty bread, to serve

Makes 2 servings (one can be frozen for another time)

Heat the oil in a large, high-sided frying pan/skillet. Add the chopped onion and garlic and cook for a few minutes over medium heat. Add the chorizo sausage and cook for a further 2–3 minutes.

Add the red wine and bring to the boil. Allow to bubble until the mixture has reduced by half. Add the tomatoes, red onion petals, butter beans, 100 ml/½ cup water and the dried mixed herbs and rosemary or thyme sprigs. Simmer, uncovered for about 10 minutes.

Season to taste with salt and pepper and spoon into a warm serving bowl. Sprinkle with the Parmesan cheese and serve immediately with chunks of warm crusty bread to mop up the juices.

This delicious *coq-au-vin*-like dish is a wonderful way to warm up on a cold day. It's worth making a batch and freezing what you don't eat for another time; alternatively, halve the quantities given here and eat the rest the next day. With the chicken bones removed, it also makes an excellent filling for an individual pie — just add a puff pastry lid.

chicken drumsticks stewed in wine with bacon and thyme

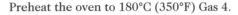

2 tablespoons vegetable oil

2 onions, halved and sliced

8 chicken drumsticks

a few sprigs of thyme

3–4 garlic cloves, sliced

85 g/⅓ cup bacon lardons

2 teaspoons salt

125 ml/½ cup dry white wine

1 bay leaf

2 tablespoons plain/all-purpose flour

2 tablespoons butter, softened

salt and freshly ground black pepper

To serve

steamed courgettes/zucchini

creamy mashed potatoes

Makes 4 servings (can be frozen for another time)

Preheat the oven to 180°C (350°F) Gas 4.

Heat the oil in a large, deep casserole dish. Add the onions and cook over medium heat until softened. Transfer to a plate, season with salt and set aside.

Add the chicken drumsticks in batches to the hot oil and cook for 5–8 minutes, turning once, until evenly browned. Transfer to a plate, season with salt and set aside.

Return the onions to the casserole dish. Add the thyme, garlic and bacon and stir to scrape up any browned bits. Cook for 2–3 minutes, until the bacon just browns. Add the salt and wine and bring to the boil. Boil for 1 minute to cook off the alcohol.

Return the browned chicken to the pan and add the bay leaf. Cover with the lid and transfer to the preheated oven. Cook for 2–2½ hours, or until the chicken is very tender. If the sauce seems too thin, mix the flour and butter together to make a paste. Remove the chicken, whisk the paste into the liquid in the pan and simmer, stirring, until it thickens. Taste and season with salt and pepper if needed. (Freeze individual portions in small foil containers at this stage, each containing 2 drumsticks and a quarter of the cooled sauce.)

Serve on a warmed serving plate with a generous amount of sauce and chopped parsley, with steamed courgettes/zucchini and creamy mashed potatoes.

Variation: For Tarragon Chicken, omit the bacon, garlic and bay leaf and stir in a large handful of chopped tarragon and a few spoonfuls of cream just before serving.

A simple and tasty supper that can be ready in no time. This curry can also be made with boneless lamb, thinly sliced beef or even boneless skinless duck breast. Most supermarkets now stock good-quality curry paste, so the ingredients should be easy to find.

thai green chicken curry

½ tablespoon vegetable oil

1 shallot (or ½ small onion), finely chopped

a small piece of fresh ginger, grated

2–3 tablespoons Thai green curry paste, to taste

400 g/14 oz. boneless, skinless chicken, preferably thigh meat, cut into bite-size pieces

400 ml/scant 1¾ cups canned coconut milk

75 ml/½ cup chicken stock

½ tablespoon soy sauce, plus extra to taste

1½ tablespoons fish sauce, plus extra to taste

150 g/1 cup mangetout/snow peas

100 g/1 cup beansprouts

leaves from ½ small bunch of coriander/cilantro, chopped

2–3 spring onions/scallions, sliced on the diagonal

To serve

cooked white rice

lime wedges

Makes 2 servings (can be frozen for another time)

Heat the oil in a large frying pan/skillet or deep sauté pan. Add the shallot or onion and cook for 3–5 minutes over a medium heat until softened and just golden. Stir in the ginger and curry paste and cook for 1 minute.

Add the chicken and cook for 2–3 minutes, stirring to coat well. Add the coconut milk and stock. Bring to the boil, reduce the heat to a simmer, cover and cook for 25–30 minutes, until the chicken is tender.

Stir in the soy sauce, fish sauce, mangetout/snow peas and beansprouts and cook for a further 2–3 minutes without the lid, until the vegetables are piping hot but still slightly crisp. Taste and adjust the seasoning, adding more soy or fish sauce as required.

Stir in half the chopped coriander/cilantro and spring onions/scallions. (Let cool and chill or freeze any you aren't using in an individual portion at this stage.)

Spoon onto a warmed serving plate. Sprinkle with the remaining spring onions/scallions and serve with rice and lime wedges for squeezing.

The colours and aromas in this dish will transport you to the south of France. Be sure to choose wrinkly, oven-dried black olives for this dish; ordinary stoned black olives simply won't do. Accompany with crusty bread and a green salad lightly dressed with a good olive oil.

roasted provençal salmon and vegetables with rouille

125 g/1 cup baby new potatoes, scrubbed and quartered

125 g/4½ oz. courgettes/zucchini, halved and quartered

½ small fennel bulb, halved and sliced

½ red bell pepper, cored, deseeded and sliced

½ yellow bell pepper, cored, deseeded and sliced

1 plum tomato, cored and quartered

½ red onion, sliced into sixths

a small pinch of saffron threads

a sprig of thyme

1 tablespoon olive oil, plus extra to drizzle

30 g/⅓ cup pitted black olives

a small handful of basil leaves, shredded

1 boneless, skinless salmon fillet (weighing about 200 g/7 oz.)

salt and freshly ground black pepper

For the rouille

50 ml/¼ cup of good-quality mayonnaise

½ garlic clove, crushed

a pinch of paprika

a pinch of cayenne pepper

Serves 1

Preheat the oven to 220°C (425°F) Gas 7.

Combine the vegetables in a large baking pan. Add the saffron and thyme and a good dose of olive oil. Toss with your hands to coat evenly. Spread the vegetables out in an even layer and sprinkle with salt. Bake in the preheated oven for 20–25 minutes, until just browned.

Meanwhile, prepare the rouille. Combine the ingredients in a small bowl, adding garlic, paprika and cayenne to taste. Mix well, adjust the seasoning if necessary, and set aside.

Remove the vegetables from the oven and sprinkle over the olives and basil. Arrange the salmon on top, drizzle a little olive oil over it and season with salt and pepper. Return to the oven and bake for about 15 minutes more, until the salmon is just cooked through. Enjoy immediately, with the rouille on the side for spooning.

The use of vodka as the poaching liquid transforms a simple salmon fillet into a distinctive dish that's ideal as a special treat. Marinating the fish in the vodka and lime for a full 10 minutes before cooking gives it a lovely citrus flavour.

vodka-poached salmon with coriander pesto

50 ml/3 tablespoons vodka

finely grated zest and freshly squeezed juice of ½ lime

1 skinless salmon fillet (weighing about 200 g/7 oz.)

salt and freshly ground black pepper

steamed, buttered green beans and mashed potoatoes, to serve

For the coriander/cilantro pesto

20 g/1 generous tablespoon pine nuts, toasted

a small bunch of coriander/cilantro

¼ red chilli/chile, deseeded and roughly chopped

1 small garlic clove

2 tablespoons extra virgin olive oil

20 g/¼ cup finely grated Parmesan cheese

1 tablespoon good-quality mayonnaise

a small food processor or mortar and pestle

Serves 1

Preheat the oven to 190°C (375°F) Gas 5.

Pour the vodka into a small, shallow, non-metallic ovenproof dish and add the lime zest and juice. Put the salmon fillet in the vodka mixture and season well with salt and pepper. Cover and set aside to marinate in a cool place for at least 10 minutes.

Meanwhile, make the pesto. Put the pine nuts, coriander/cilantro, chilli/chile and garlic in the bowl of a small food processor or mortar and pestle. Blitz or pound until evenly chopped, then add the olive oil in a thin stream with the motor running until smooth. Transfer to a bowl and stir in the grated Parmesan cheese and mayonnaise. (Any leftover pesto would be delicious tossed through some cooked pasta with slow-roast cherry tomatoes.)

Cover the salmon with foil and bake in the preheated oven for 6–7 minutes, or until just tender. Remove the salmon from the oven and discard the poaching liquid. Arrange the salmon fillet on a mound of steamed green beans with some creamy mashed potatoes and spoon a little of the pesto over the top. Enjoy immediately.

Although wonderful with tuna, the salsa verde is also delicious with grilled/broiled chicken, so you could double the quantities and keep some covered in the fridge for the next evening.

tuna steak with warm potato salad and salsa verde

½ tablespoon extra virgin olive oil, plus extra to serve

1 fresh tuna steak (weighing about 150 g/5 oz.)

salt and freshly ground black pepper

a few spinach leaves, to serve

For the potato salad

100 g/¾ cup baby new potatoes, scrubbed

2 tablespoons extra virgin olive oil

freshly squeezed juice of ¼ lemon

½ teaspoon wholegrain mustard

½ teaspoon chopped chives

sea salt

For the salsa verde

15 g/½ oz. flat-leaf parsley, chopped

½ tablespoon capers, drained, rinsed and chopped

1 anchovy fillet, soaked in milk, drained and finely chopped

1 small garlic clove, crushed

a handful of green olives, pitted and chopped

20 ml/1¼ tablespoons extra virgin olive oil

freshly ground black pepper

Serves 1

First, make the potato salad. Cook the potatoes in a pan of boiling salted water until they are just tender – about 15–20 minutes. Meanwhile, pour the olive oil into a medium bowl and add the lemon juice, mustard and chives. Whisk to form a dressing.

Drain the cooked potatoes and wait until they are cool enough to handle before cutting them into thick slices (or halves if they are very small). Toss them in the dressing until they are thoroughly coated. Set aside.

Combine all the ingredients for the salsa verde in a small bowl and mix well. Taste for seasoning and add a little pepper if needed.

Brush the olive oil over the tuna steak and season well with salt and pepper. Heat a non-stick frying pan/skillet over a high heat, add and cook the tuna for 2 minutes on each side, turning only once.

Remove from the pan and cut the tuna into smaller pieces. Arrange the warm potato salad on a plate and top with the tuna. Spoon the salsa verde over the top. Serve with spinach leaves dressed with a drizzle of extra virgin olive oil.

This festive and aromatic curry freezes well in small batches and
is a warming treat to have on hand for lunches or light meals.
Serve with steamed couscous or rice.

chickpea curry with coconut and tamarind

370 g/2 cups dried chickpeas

1¼ tablespoons black mustard seeds

1¼ tablespoons cumin seeds

6 tablespoons vegetable oil

2 garlic cloves, crushed

4 tablespoons desiccated coconut/dried shredded coconut

2 tablespoons sesame seeds

2 tablespoons chickpea/gram flour

½ teaspoon ground turmeric

½ teaspoon dried chilli/hot pepper flakes

1 fresh green chilli/chile, deseeded and finely chopped

200 ml/1 cup passata (Italian sieved tomatoes)

3 tablespoons tamarind concentrate

200 g/1 cup dates, pitted and finely chopped

1½ teaspoons salt

2 tablespoons sugar

To serve

plain yogurt

chopped coriander/cilantro

Makes 6 servings (can be frozen for another time)

Put the chickpeas in a bowl, cover with cold water and leave to soak overnight. The next day, discard the soaking water. Re-cover the chickpeas with fresh water and place the pan over a high heat on the stove. Bring to the boil, skim off any froth that rises to the surface and simmer gently for 50–60 minutes, or until tender. Drain and set aside.

Put the mustard and cumin seeds in a small frying pan/skillet and toast over a low heat until the seeds become aromatic and begin to pop. Set aside to cool.

Heat the oil in a large saucepan, casserole dish or deep sauté pan. Add the garlic, coconut, sesame seeds, chickpea/gram flour, turmeric, dried chilli/hot pepper flakes and fresh chilli/chile and cook over a medium heat for 2–3 minutes, until aromatic.

Stir in the passata, tamarind, dates, 2 tablespoons of the toasted mustard and cumin seeds (reserving the rest to serve), cooked chickpeas, half the coriander/cilantro and 1 litre/4 cups water. Mix together well.

Bring to the boil, reduce the heat to simmer and cook, covered, on low heat for about 50 minutes, stirring occasionally.

Stir in the salt and sugar. Taste and adjust the seasoning as necessary. (Let cool and freeze any you aren't using in individual portions at this stage.)

Enjoy warm or at room temperature, topped with plain yogurt and sprinkled with chopped coriander/cilantro and the reserved toasted cumin and mustard seeds. (Once toasted these will keep in an airtight container for several weeks.)

chapter 6

treat yourself

sweet and indulgent desserts

Figs roasted in the oven with a splash of warming alcohol positively ooze succulence and sweetness. The voluptuous Greek yogurt is so stiff you could stand a spoon in it, and it becomes gorgeously fudgy when scattered with rich muscovado sugar.

figs roasted in Madeira with pine nuts and fudgy Greek yogurt

2 fresh figs

2 tablespoons Madeira

a small handful of pine nuts

1 tablespoon dark muscovado sugar

50 g/¼ cup thick Greek yogurt

Serves 1

Preheat the oven to 200°C (400°F) Gas 6.

Cut the stalks off the figs and cut a cross in the top about one-third of the way through. Stand them in a baking pan, pour over the Madeira and scatter with the pine nuts and half the sugar. Bake for 15–20 minutes, basting occasionally.

Spoon the yogurt into a bowl and sprinkle with the remaining sugar. Leave to stand for 10 minutes until it absorbs the sugar and turns slightly fudgy in texture.

When the figs are cooked and on the verge of collapsing gracefully, transfer them to the bowl next to the fudgy yogurt and pour over the hot sticky juices. Eat immediately.

This is the ultimate in simple puddings, and if you have these ingredients in your fridge, freezer and storecupboard, you'll never be caught out by a sweet craving. The secret is to make sure that the summer fruits are just frozen before pouring over the hot white chocolate sauce.

iced summer berries with hot white chocolate sauce

125 g/1 cup frozen mixed summer berries (such as blueberries, strawberries, raspberries, blackberries and redcurrants)

50 g/2½ oz. good-quality white chocolate, roughly chopped

50 ml/¼ cup single/light cream

½ teaspoon runny honey

Serves 1

Remove the summer berries from the freezer 10 minutes before you want to serve them.

Put the white chocolate, cream and honey in a small heatproof bowl. Fill a small pan with cold water and bring it to a simmer. Place the bowl over the pan, but make sure that the base does not touch the water. Gently heat, stirring continuously with a rubber or wooden spatula, until the chocolate is melted and you have a smooth sauce. Alternatively, you can melt the chocolate with the cream and honey in the microwave. Place them in a small bowl and microwave for a few seconds until smooth and runny. Be careful: white chocolate scorches easily, so don't overcook it.

Arrange the semi-frozen berries on a serving plate, then pour the hot white chocolate sauce all over them so that the heat of the sauce begins to melt and soften them. Serve immediately.

Variation: The hot white chocolate sauce is also delicious spooned over balls of dark chocolate ice cream or poured over chopped fudge brownies and bananas.

The sweet and frothy egg mixture spread on top of the fruit is
called a sabayon, and makes this a very easy and elegant dessert.
It's best when made with a bit of something alcoholic — a sweet
wine such as Muscat de Beaumes de Venise is nice.

berry and sabayon gratin

150 g/1¼ cups frozen mixed
berries, thawed

1 large egg yolk and 2 egg whites

20 g/1¼ tablespoons
caster/superfine sugar

¼ tablespoon runny honey

30 ml/2 tablespoons sweet
dessert wine (optional)

½ tablespoon icing/
confectioners' sugar

a shallow ovenproof gratin dish

Serves 1

Place the fruit in a small gratin dish. Preheat the grill/broiler
to high.

Bring a saucepan of water just to simmering point. Choose a
heatproof bowl (glass is ideal) that will sit tightly on top of the
saucepan. Put the egg yolk and sugar in the bowl and whisk, off
the heat, until blended. Transfer the bowl to the saucepan and
continue whisking, over the heat, until the mixture is thick and
frothy, about 2–4 minutes. Don't let the water boil. Whisk in the
honey and wine, if using, then remove from the heat.

Beat the egg whites in another bowl until they hold stiff peaks.

Gently fold the beaten whites into the warm yolk mixture until
blended. Spread the mixture evenly over the fruit in the gratin.
Lightly sprinkle the top with a dusting of icing/confectioners'
sugar. Cook under the hot grill/broiler until just browned,
about 1–2 minutes (watch carefully because it will
colour quite quickly). Eat immediately.

Variation: Use fresh berries when in season.
Raspberries/blackberries and strawberries are best,
mixed or on their own.

Most evenings, a bowl of fruit salad, a piece of ripe seasonal fruit or a square of chocolate is all you need to finish off your meal. But sometimes on a weekend night you need to treat yourself, and these speedy desserts are the solution.

quick desserts

hot fudge sauce

Melt 60 g/2½ oz. good-quality dark chocolate in a pan with 2 tablespoons strong black coffee. Once melted, add 1 tablespoon butter, 1 tablespoon double/heavy cream and ½ teaspoon cinnamon. Scoop balls of your favourite vanilla ice cream into a dish, pour over the luscious warm sauce and dig in! If there's any left over, cover and keep in the fridge.

raspberry banana split

Push 50 g/scant ½ cup raspberries through a fine-meshed, non-metallic sieve and stir in 1 tablespoon icing/confectioners' sugar to make a sauce. Peel and halve a banana and put it on a serving plate. Add 2–3 balls of good-quality vanilla or strawberry ice cream, top with a handful of fresh raspberries and drizzle with the raspberry sauce. Sprinkle with toasted and chopped nuts such as macadamias, almonds, hazelnuts or peanuts.

speedy apricot fool

Use 100 g/3½ oz. bottled apricot compote and mix with 50 ml/¼ cup ready-made custard or crème Anglaise and 50 ml/¼ cup whipped double/heavy cream. Spoon into a glass and decorate with toasted nuts. You could use other fruit compotes such as rhubarb, gooseberry or cherry in the same way.

strawberry and passion fruit meringue crush

Mash ½ punnet of strawberries with a dash of sugar, then fold in 25 g/1 oz. broken ready-made meringue nests and 3 tablespoons lightly whipped cream. Spoon into a sundae glass and top with the pulp of 1 passion fruit.

sparkling sorbet cup

This should be reserved for a really special occasion! In a martini glass, place a scoop of best-quality blackberry or mango sorbet. Sprinkle with mixed berries (such as raspberries, strawberries or blueberries) and slowly and carefully pour a little sparkling wine into the glass (you can buy a small individual bottle of Prosecco or Cava for this purpose!). Enjoy immediately.

cheat's chocolate 'tartufo'

Put a chocolate-covered honeycomb bar in a freezer bag and bash using the end of a rolling pin until finely crushed. Scoop rich chocolate ice cream into 2 balls and roll in the crushed honeycomb crumbs. Place on a baking sheet covered with parchment paper and freeze for 2 hours before serving.

ice cream cookie sandwich

Mix together a little shredded coconut or desiccated coconut with some finely chopped toasted hazelnuts or almonds and put on a small plate. Scoop 2 balls of softened vanilla fudge- or toffee whirl-flavoured ice cream onto 2 small chocolate chip cookies. Top with 2 more cookies and gently press down, pushing the ice cream to the edge. Roll the ice cream in the nut-coconut mixture and eat immediately, or make and freeze ahead and remove the cookie sandwiches 5 minutes before you want to eat them, to soften.

easy mango granita

This is a refreshing and healthy end to a meal. Peel a large, ripe mango, cut away the flesh and put it in a food processor. Purée with the juice of ½ lime. Taste and add more juice if necessary. Pour into a shallow freezerproof dish and freeze overnight. To serve, use a spoon to scrape the frozen mango into 'icicle shards' and fill a chilled martini glass. Eat as soon as possible.

blueberry and lemon parfait

Crush 3 shortbread biscuits/cookies into fine crumbs. Mix with 1 tablespoon melted butter. Put half of this mixture into a wine glass. Mix together 1 tablespoon lemon curd with 75 ml/⅓ cup Greek yogurt and spoon a layer on top of the shortbread mixture. Top with a scattering of blueberries. Repeat the layers until the glass is full.

grilled pineapple with vodka

Cut off the top and bottom of ½ large ripe pineapple and cut off the skin in long, thin strips. Use a sharp knife to remove the 'eyes'. Slice into quarters lengthways and remove the core. Lay the pineapple on a baking sheet and drizzle with 50 ml/2 oz. lemon vodka. Season with freshly ground black pepper. Place under a hot grill for 5 minutes until golden, then serve with lemon sorbet.

simple summer berry brûlée

Place 60 g/½ cup mixed summer berries in a serving bowl. Mix together 1 tablespoon each crème fraîche and fromage frais with ¼ teaspoon vanilla extract and spoon over the fruits. Sprinkle each with 1 tablespoon soft brown sugar. Leave in the fridge overnight. The sugar magically melts into a caramelized brûlée-style coating.

This is such a simple but delicious dessert that you feel it must be bad for you. In fact, fresh fruit and fragrant honey are all that are needed to make this so good, so why not treat yourself to a large scoop of vanilla ice cream on the side!

peaches poached in vanilla honey syrup

½ tablespoon runny honey, orange-blossom if available

¼ vanilla pod/bean, sliced lengthways

1 ripe peach, unpeeled, stoned/pitted and halved

30 g/¼ cup fresh raspberries

vanilla ice cream, to serve (optional)

Serves 1

Put 60 ml/¼ cup water, the honey and vanilla pod/bean in a large saucepan. Bring to the boil over high heat, then reduce the heat, cover and simmer gently for 5 minutes to allow the vanilla to impart its flavour.

Add the peach halves and return to the boil. Continue to simmer for 3–4 minutes, or until the peach halves are soft. Remove them from the pan with a slotted spoon.

While the peach halves cool for a few minutes, boil the remaining syrup in the pan until it has reduced by about half.

When the peach halves are cool enough to handle, peel off their skins, which should come off like little jackets. Serve in a bowl with some raspberries and drizzle with the syrup. Serve with a large scoop of vanilla ice cream, if liked.

This individual fruity dessert contains the healthy addition of oats and sunflower seeds in the crumble topping. If rhubarb is not in season, plums, apple and blackberries are equally delicious. The crumbles can be frozen, uncooked, for up to three months.

rhubarb, pear and ginger crumble

175 g/6 oz. rhubarb, sliced into bite-size pieces

1 pear, peeled, cored and cut into bite-size pieces

5 tablespoons freshly squeezed orange juice

1 tablespoon soft light brown sugar

1 teaspoon ground ginger

For the crumble topping

100 g/¾ cup plain/all-purpose flour

40 g/½ cup whole porridge/rolled oats

1 tablespoon sunflower seeds

60 g/⅓ cup demerara sugar

70 g/⅓ cup cold butter, cubed

chilled cream or vanilla ice cream, to serve (optional)

4 individual heatproof ramekins

Makes 4 servings (can be frozen for another time)

Preheat the oven to 200°C (400°F) Gas 6.

Put the rhubarb, pear, orange juice, sugar and ginger in a large bowl and stir until everything is combined. Pack the fruit and any juice into 4 individual heatproof dishes until the fruit nearly reaches the top.

To make the crumble, put the flour, oats, seeds, sugar and butter in a mixing bowl and rub them together with your fingertips until they form a coarse, chunky breadcrumb texture – you don't want the crumble topping to be too fine in texture. Sprinkle the crumble mixture over the fruit. Wrap 3 in foil and freeze them at this stage to cook and enjoy another time.

Put the dishes on a baking sheet and bake the crumbles for 25–30 minutes, or until the tops are golden. Serve with chilled cream for pouring or a scoop of vanilla ice cream.

index

recipe credits

Laura Washburn
Berry sabayon gratin
Bolognese sauce
Chicken and chorizo quesadilla
Chicken drumsticks stewed in wine with bacon and thyme
Chickpea curry with coconut and tamarind
Chicory gratin with ham and blue cheese
Chilli bacon swiss cheese sandwich
Chipotle, black bean and feta quesadilla
Chorizo, bean and pepper burrito
Courgette gratin with fresh herbs and goat cheese
Hot halloumi and falafel wrap with tahini sauce
Ham and egg breakfast quesadilla
Ham hock and smoked mozzarella rigatoni
Minestrone
Peaches poached in vanilla honey syrup
Prawn and feta pasta bake Roasted
Provencal salmon and vegetables with rouille
Salmon, basil and Parmesan pasta bake
Seafood curry
Shredded chicken tacos
Smoked trout hash with horseradish cream
Spicy corn mac n' cheese
Spicy lamb meatball tagine
Tandoori chicken and paneer stuffed naan with mango chutney
Thai green chicken curry
Ultimate three-cheese toastie

Caroline Marsden
Beetroot, walnut and warm goat cheese salad
Blackened salmon salad
Coconut Thai chicken salad
Deli pasta spread pages 60–61
Flavoured butters pages 112–113
Gravadlax and picked cucumber open sandwich
Iced summer berries with hot white chocolate sauce
Curry glazed pork escalope with spiced potatoes and peas
Pappardelle with artichoke hearts and Parma ham
Pear, blue cheese and croute salad
Salad dressings pages 44–45
Smoked trout, warm new potato and beetroot salad
Spanish sausage and butter bean tagine
Tagliatelle with broccoli, anchovy, Parmesan and crème fraîche
Tuna steak with warm potato salad and salsa verde
Quick desserts pages 136–137
Vodka poached salmon with coriander pesto

Tonia George
Chicken and lentil curry with cucumber yogurt
Chunky puy lentil and vegetable soup
Figs roasted in Madeira with pine nuts and fudgy Greek yogurt
Garlic mushrooms and goat cheese on sourdough toast
Herby sausages with polenta and redcurrant gravy
Mint tea couscous with roast squash, halloumi, dates and pistachios
Minty pea risotto soup
Pad Thai
Tagliatelle with peas and goat cheese pesto

Chloe Coker & Jane Montgomery
French toast stuffed with banana
Granola with berry compote
Honey and apricot breakfast muffins
Potato and celeriac rosti with spinach

Nadia Arumugam
Beef chow mein
Chicken pad Thai
Green curry fried rice with chicken, green beans and peas
Wok tossed jasmine rice with crabmeat and asparagus

Miranda Ballard
Big breakfast burger
Cheesy root vegetable burgers
Chilli con Carne burger

Ghillie Basan
Chicken tandoori kebabs
Monkfish kebabs with chermoula

Fiona Beckett
Cooking steak: the basics
Teriyaki steak with noodles

Annie Rigg
Chargrilled halloumi with mixed olive and herb tapenade

Tori Haschka
Sangria prawn salad

Nicola Graimes
Rhubarb, pear and ginger crumble

picture credits